Fitness Swimming

Fitness Swimming

Lifetime Programs

JOSEPH E. MCEVOY, D. P. E.

Aquatics Director, Dickinson College
Carlisle, PA

Illustrations by Kim Dickerson

PRINCETON BOOK COMPANY, PUBLISHERS
PRINCETON, NEW JERSEY

Design by Design and Illustration
Typesetting by Delmas
Copyright © 1985 by
Princeton Book Company, Publishers
All rights reserved

Library of Congress Catalog Card Number 84-62820
ISBN 916622-34-7
Printed in the United States of America

This book is respectfully dedicated to my parents. In 1954, they pledged $35 toward the construction of a municipal swimming pool in Livingston, New Jersey. That small investment provided wonderful opportunities for me as a young person and ultimately led to a highly satisfying career in introducing other people to the benefits of swimming.

Contents

FOREWORD

Habits are hard to break, so it was a long time before I gave up merely chattering about how nice it would be to swim during the noon hour and instead actually went trudging over to the college pool. It was an intimidating experience. The pool was only open to adult swimmers for brief periods of time each day, and then only if a lifeguard remembered to show up. I could manage a dozen lengths or so if I stayed with the sidestroke and the elementary backstroke, but the crawl was a killer. Worse yet, no one seemed to care when I triumphantly swam two lengths without stopping. Not that I wanted a brass band or a commemorative plaque, but a word of encouragement would have helped. So it was not surprising that I quit swimming after a couple of weeks.

It was two more years before I found my way back to the gym and into the pool. This time, at least, I had three friends with me. We still had plenty of problems—aching muscles we didn't know we had, water in the ear and up the nose, and wet towels steaming up the locker—but sharing these miseries helped turn them into funny moments or trivial nuisances. Nonetheless the swimming was still basically a discouraging experience. We didn't seem to accomplish anything, despite our efforts, and a vague disquiet gradually replaced our hopes for fun in the water.

Then one day Joe McEvoy appeared. As if by magic the college pool was open for as long each day as the library. Lifeguards were always on time. A friendly voice could be counted on to give encouragement, to suggest an improvement here or there, to hint at fresh possibilities, and to set our aspirations higher. I still remember the day I was told flat out to swim 20 lengths. I'd never done more than 4 at a time before then, although I harbored a secret goal of doing 10 in a row. But Coach Joe said 20, so why not? And I survived to brag about it for days afterward.

We now have a full-fledged and excitingly varied program for adult lap swimmers. This book describes the steps by which each of us was led from an initial knock on McEvoy's door to a level of involvement that could become as rigorous as Masters-level competition but that most certainly included membership in Joe's famous Fitness Swimming Club. The adults who regularly dip their toes in our pool come from all walks of life: college faculty and staff, business and professional people from the town, homemakers, retired folk, students from the law school. Some are in the water at 9:00 each morning and others swim only at night, but the most popular time is over the noon hour.

I'm a noon-hour type myself, and I've got lots of comrades now and lots of camaraderie. Our motivation is always the same: swimming laps is good for us. Our bodies like the exercise and we like each other's company. Our emotions are cooled by the rhythmic relaxation, our thoughts are allowed to wander creatively, and our drive for accomplishment is given a pleasing outlet. Sandwiches on the pool patio are a social highlight. Even the walk to the gym is an opportunity to wind down from the morning's tensions and warm up one's muscles in preparation for the day's workout.

Swimming laps illustrates the important truth that education is a lifelong adventure, that it is deeply satisfying to perfect old skills and acquire new ones. The standards of excellence in swimming are a blend of individualized self-surpassing goals and general goals appropriate to all people of similar age or ability. Thus there is something marvelously democratic about a swimming pool. When everyone is dressed in a swimsuit it is hard to be pretentious or to pull rank. People who excel in one aspect of swimming meet others whose achievements lie in some other aspect, and there is plenty for each one to learn from everyone else. Swimming also requires total involvement. In the water, enjoying your harmony with its buoyancy, using its resistance to propel yourself forward, you are no longer fragmented into mind and body, thinker and doer. You discover yourself as someone who at once thinks, feels, wills, and acts.

Like the library, the swimming pool is a resource for those who wish to be educated, who seek life's fullness by enlarging their awareness of the world's possibilities and their own capacities. Coach Joe's book is a guided tour through that library. Read it with caution, because if you stay with it to the end you will be hooked on swimming for the rest of your life. Eventually, if you don't watch out, you will begin to grow webbing between the toes.

When my friends and I had at long last swum the required 100 miles, we were eligible to become full-fledged members of the Fitness Swimming Club. We celebrated on the outdoor patio beside the pool by festooning a crate with tablecloth and candelabrum. Champagne and caviar were served, in celebration of our transformation from mere water churners into bona fide lap swimmers. A couple of years later, several of us contracted to "swim the English Channel" over the semester break. Each half mile or mile we logged in the pool was translated onto a huge wall chart monitoring our progress from Dover to Calais. We urged each other on, warning about ships and jellyfish and other swimmers, noting when the white cliffs could no longer be seen and when the rocks of Cape Gris-Nez were first sighted. We commemorated everyone's completion of the 21-mile swim by preparing a full-course French dinner, lacking only truffles to give it a five-star rating.

Such fantasies and their celebration may seem mere foolishness, but they are at the same time profound occasions. In such play we celebrate the wonder of being human. In our noontime recreation we prepare ourselves for the deeper triumphs and challenges of life. I can't imagine a better way to spend an hour each day. I hope you will soon be joining us.

George Allan
Dean of the College
Dickinson College
January 1985

PREFACE

I was first exposed to the idea of swimming for fitness in the early 1960s as a lifeguard and Water Safety Instructor. Each summer, a huge chart would be posted in the pool office at Memorial Pool in Livingston, New Jersey, and some of the regular patrons would try to complete 50 miles in the American Red Cross Swim and Stay Fit program. At the time, the distance seemed impossibly long, and the whole idea seemed crazy to me. I thought it was funny to watch someone do a "cannonball" by the side of one of these lap-swimmers, and then swim away quickly underwater, having interrupted the lap-swimmer's workout for the tenth time that day. I really didn't understand what these lap-swimmers were doing.

As a freshman at Springfield College in 1965–66, I first read about swimming for fitness (one of the areas of expression in swimming) and organic condition (one of the factors that control swimming success) in the 1960 edition of Charles E. Silvia's *Manual* (121, pp. 4–5)*. This manual accompanied the basic swimming course, and was the start of my aquatics education there. I began to understand more about swimming being the "best" exercise, but it would be 11 more years before I tried it myself and began to prepare notes for this book.

A landmark publication for me was Kenneth Cooper's *Aerobics* (34) in 1968. Although it emphasized jogging and running (but included some swimming), it marked a transition in physical fitness from a strength orientation to a cardiovascular orientation (or, it's better to have a healthy heart than big biceps). Cooper explained exercise theory in popular terms, and directed people into planned, progressive training programs. It was an important step forward when the average person began talking about cardiovascular conditioning, training effects, heart rates, 12-minute tests, and 30 points a week. Yet, I remember wondering why those who ran so

---

* The method of footnoting used in this book is as follows: the first number in the parentheses refers to a numbered source in the References and Further Readings; if specific material was cited, it can be found on the page numbers listed.

well and were models of aerobic fitness didn't always do so well in the swimming pool.

I completed a valuable apprenticeship in aquatics at Springfield College from 1965 to 1975 and at Pine Knoll Swim School in Springfield, Massachusetts, from 1970 to 1975. The principal guidance in my aquatics education was provided by Professor Silvia, the swimming coach at the college and the director of the summer swim school. This educational environment was my first exposure to such fundamental procedures as bobbing and breathing exercises, interval workouts, turns and push-offs, and virtually all aspects of competitive swimming. Most importantly, Coach Silvia was a master of stroke technique. He described the movements of the upper extremities in most of the strokes in kinesiological and anatomical terms (119, pp. 11–14, and 120, p. 70), which represents a unique approach to the field of competitive swimming, and is at the core of understanding highly skilled swimming performance. The stroke descriptions in this book build upon this scientific base in a greatly simplified manner.

I began my own personal fitness swimming program and started to prepare this book in 1976 while teaching at the University of Georgia. The original fitness swimming course was designed in 1976–77 as a parallel to the jogging course there, and was first taught in 1978. High enrollments and positive student reactions made it obvious that this course was a good addition to the basic physical education program and that fitness swimming was a vast untapped market for teachers and students.

When I started teaching at Dickinson College in 1979, I encountered a small but eager group of faculty swimmers. Their enthusiasm eventually led to the whole spectrum of activities within the Fitness Swimming Club. My main thrust in curriculum development has been to establish additional fitness swimming courses in a "self-paced" or "independent study" format, which has brought fitness swimming to a larger number of students than would be possible in conventional scheduling. The principles I have worked with as a designer and instructor of these fitness swimming courses are set forth in this book. Some of the highlights are:

- a discussion of the psychological benefits of the activity;
- advice on getting started;
- basic exercise theory to help you decide how often, how long, and how hard to exercise, and how to keep it interesting;
- a solid progression for learning to breathe to either side in the crawl stroke;
- a discussion of two methods of training (continuous swimming and interval training) and the presentation of workouts in three different formats (lap-swimming, timed, and interval workouts);
- how to use equipment;

- workout variations to make your program more interesting;
- descriptions of strokes and turns to help you learn new skills or refine old ones;
- a chapter on Masters Swimming for those with competitive goals;
- a progressive series of seven courses for independent study;
- an invitation to join the Dickinson College Fitness Swimming Club and to take part in some of its activities and challenges;
- the Fitness Swimming Hotline, on which you can talk to me about your questions and problems; and
- review sections, appearing at the end of most chapters, that take the form of either self-testing questions or a checklist of skills.

This book contains some chapters on broad topics such as basic exercise theory and other chapters on specific in-the-water skills such as how to breathe or how to do a turn. A good model to follow when reading this book would be to read a little, swim a little, read a little more, and swim a little more. The goal is to establish a progressive program for yourself as quickly as possible. At the beginning, you do not need to understand every detail of this book, and you do not need to be a great swimmer. Read the book and relate to as much as you possibly can, then get in the pool and complete some workouts. You will be amazed 6 months from now at how well these ideas and skills can all fit together for you in an exciting and challenging fitness swimming training program, the type of program that you can maintain for the rest of your life. Good luck and enjoy yourself!

ACKNOWLEDGMENTS

Harry Albee, Pam Albee, Betsy Allan, George Allan, Dan Bechtel, Joan Bechtel, Gladys Fusselman, Marlin Gibb, Penny Gulden, Marvin Israel, Mary Margaret Kellogg, Bob Leyon, Mary Anne Morefield, Anne Olmstead, and Mike Sienkiewicz have been stellar members of the Fitness Swimming Club at Dickinson College. Without always realizing it, they have "field-tested" many of the procedures and concepts in this book, and I am extremely grateful for their responsiveness, good spirits, and willingness to try new ideas.

As the first president of the Fitness Swimming Club, George Allan also wrote the Foreword to this book. Characteristically, George's blend of concepts and anecdotes leads us to the deeper meaning of this activity and takes us far beyond just swimming laps.

David Watkins, Athletic Director and Chairman of the Physical Education Department at Dickinson College, has been totally supportive of this project. Several years ago, Dave shared with me the courses which he taught here in a self-paced format, and this was the origin of the fitness swimming courses presented in this book in Chapter 10.

Kim Ruehle Dickerson, a former swimmer at the University of Georgia, is a talented illustrator who developed a visual presentation of the complexities of the various strokes, turns, and breathing exercises. Her illustrations are a valuable complement to the written descriptions in this book.

My wife, Pat McEvoy, served as unofficial proofreader and editor. Her continued support and constructive criticisms were the most important contributions made by anyone to this project.

CHAPTER ONE
Introduction

This book is designed as a comprehensive source for those who would like to use swimming as a fitness activity. It builds on 9 years of "field testing" with a wide variety of college-age and adult fitness swimmers, and it describes the options available for the training programs of fitness swimmers so that they can maintain interest and stay with the activity for a long period of time.

BENEFITS OF FITNESS SWIMMING

People exercise for different reasons, and a list of these reasons would be long, diverse, and sometimes conflicting. Fitness swimmers should personalize their reasons for exercising by considering the following questions: Why am I doing it? Why should I do it? What am I getting out of it? What should I get out of it? The physical and mental benefits described here will help answer the "should" part of these questions.

PHYSICAL ASPECTS

Responses to Exercise When you swim or do any type of exercise, certain *immediate* responses will occur in your body: your heart rate and breathing rate will increase, your digestion will slow down, and your blood supply will shift to the working muscles. Unless you're in extremely cold water, you'll even sweat when you swim. In other words, all of the systems of your body mobilize automatically to react to the increased physical demands of the activity.

If you embark on a planned fitness swimming program, you will gradually create certain *long-range* responses in your body:

- The efficiency of your heart and lungs will improve.
- Your blood vessels will increase in size and number.
- Your total blood volume will be greater.
- Your blood vessels will have greater tone and elasticity.

1

- Your capacity to use oxygen during exertion will be greater.
- Your ability to relax will be improved.
- Your resting heart rate will be lowered.
- Your resting blood pressure will be lowered.
- Your general muscle tone will improve.
- Your joint and muscular flexibility will be greater.
- You may experience weight loss if you combine your exercise with dietary/life-style changes.

All of these long-term factors are known as the "training effect" (34, pp. 12 and 86), but you must exercise long enough, hard enough, and frequently enough to create these desirable changes.

Heart Disease While it is hoped that vigorous exercise can help prevent heart disease, this relationship is suggested but not absolutely certain (53, 59, 61, 102). Many factors predispose an individual to heart disease, including high blood pressure, being overweight, smoking, high cholesterol and diet, lack of exercise, and heredity. Some of these factors are controllable, but a great deal depends on when you begin to control them and to what extent, how much damage has already been done, and what the relative influence is of the less controllable factors.

Some authorities have stated that a certain system of exercise, or the ability to complete certain long-distance events, will guarantee immunity from a heart attack. This is false advertising but has great public appeal because it dwells on deep-seated fears which motivate some people to exercise. According to Kenneth Cooper: "To my knowledge, there is still nothing known to man that is completely protective against coronary heart disease—not medicine, surgery, or even marathon running" (35, p. 7).

However, exercise is positively related to surviving a heart attack. Exercise promotes the development of collateral circulation around and within the heart muscle itself, and this additional blood supply can significantly improve a heart attack victim's chances of survival and recovery.

Longevity Another hopeful myth has developed connecting exercise with a long life, and, here again, this relationship is suggested but not certain (53, 59, 61, 102). There are too many exceptions even to make this a general rule, such as the highly fit person who dies suddenly at a young age or the 100-year-old who still drinks whiskey and smokes cigarettes daily. Many factors blend together to determine our life span, and excercise is one of them but certainly not the whole picture. This relationship is clarified by the saying: "While exercise may not add years to your life, it will add life to your years."

Special Effects of Exercising in Water Water is a unique medium in which to exercise (90, p. 2). The factor of buoyancy greatly reduces weight-bearing stress on joints and muscles, providing more gentle exercise than some other fitness activities. Water provides its own high resistance to movement through it, permitting a high level of exercise with relatively slow movements and slow total body velocity. The pressure of the water, its cool temperature, and the usual horizontal position of the swimmer assist in the return of blood to the heart during activity. The cool temperature and high conductivity of water helps to remove heat from the body during exercise.

PSYCHOLOGICAL ASPECTS

Enjoyment Fitness swimming is fun, an activity you can look forward to and enjoy several times a week. To some, this value is justification enough for participation, and they regard any deep-seated physiological benefits simply as bonuses above and beyond this primary factor of enjoyment.

Some people look upon exercise as drudgery, as a daily duty or necessity, or as a sort of punishment for other aspects of their life-style. They have no perception of the *joy* that is present in this factor of enjoyment. Others exercise with a joyful and playful spirit, with a sense of wonder about their physical capacities, and with a sincere gratitude that they are alive and able to be active.

Accomplishment You can achieve a tremendous feeling of accomplishment by planning and regularly completing a vigorous fitness swimming training program. The learning of new skills, the development of your stamina, and the periodic challenging of your swimming abilities can make a large, positive contribution to your self-image and self-confidence. Short-term and long-range goals can be set and achieved as you test your physical and mental limits.

"Feel Better Response" Most fitness swimmers report that they feel better when they swim regularly; this has been called the "feel better response" (64, p. 182). People feel that they are more alert and have more energy throughout the day when they are involved in an exercise routine. There are bumper stickers that proclaim: "It feels good to feel fit" (61, p. 15). This effect is probably not long-lasting, but it may provide a strong incentive for some people to exercise frequently.

Change of Pace Fitness swimming can provide a periodic change of pace from the regular routines of your daily life. Many people feel that they return to normal responsibilities with a fresh and invigorated attitude after exercising. But you must leave your problems outside the pool or they'll ruin your workout as well. According to Hans Selye:

> You must find something to put in the place of worrying thoughts to chase them away.... If ... a person undertakes some strenuous task which needs all his attention, he may still not forget his worries, but they will certainly fade. Nothing erases unpleasant thoughts more effectively than conscious concentration on pleasant ones. (118, p. 268)

Tension Reduction Vigorous exercise activates the most fundamental systems of the body, which may not be utilized very often in daily life in our society today. For example, the sympathetic division of the autonomic nervous system automatically prepares the body for "fight or flight" (*32*, p. 139). Because we can't always fight or run away from a stressful situation in the civilized world, the body's reaction to stress is frequently blocked, resulting in a state of tension (anxiety, depression, or unexpressed anger).

The tension reduction theory maintains that exercise provides an outlet and release from physical and emotional tensions by using these normal stress responses in big-muscle activity and total body movement. This effect is a temporary one, and tensions may rebuild again before the next exercise period. According to William Morgan, "the greatest benefit of exercise is maintenance of mental health and prevention of emotional problems" (*54*, pp. 2-B, and *103*).

Isolation For some people, their daily workout is a very private and personal time. No one can talk to you while you're swimming—you're on your own in a cushioned environment. At last, you have a chance to do something for yourself and by yourself. Of course, there are social aspects to exercise and swimming, and it is good to work out with a partner or in a small group from time to time. But to get from one end of the pool to the other, ultimately you go by yourself and under your own power—and this type of self-reliance is a real treat for some fitness swimmers.

"Swimmer's High" "Swimmer's high" is the H_2O parallel to what has commonly been referred to as runner's high. It involves a greatly heightened sense of well-being while swimming, a feeling that you and the activity blend together with no apparent effort, a feeling that you are in perfect harmony with the water rather than struggling against it. These feelings have also been summarized in the word "flow" (*57*) and involve a centering of attention on the activity and an alteration in your normal senses of time, space, and self. The types and intensities of responses depend on how completely and how long you are immersed in your exercise. This mental state will either happen or not—you can't force it or will it to occur. The frequency of this phenomenon varies greatly from swimmer to swimmer—but remember, this won't happen every time you swim down the pool.

Exercise Addiction For a few people, the psychological benefits become abnormally important and they become "addicted" to exercise (*84*, p. 73). They may work out two or three times a day. Exercise begins to dominate their life-style, becoming more important than their work, family, and social activities. Exercise addicts suffer from delusions of invincibility (*21*). They will ignore serious injuries and disregard advice to slow down or stop their exercise. When deprived of exercise, they experience withdrawal-type symptoms. "The exercise addict finds himself in much

4

the same place as the alcoholic or heroin addict. Feeling good becomes more important than anything else" (104, p. 62). This is a relatively recent phenomenon, and its treatment should involve some kind of psychological counseling.

WHY NOT EXERCISE?

According to *The Perrier Study: Fitness in America*, people use any or all of nine arguments to justify not starting a regular exercise program:

1. "I'm so busy that I don't have enough energy left when I get around to thinking about exercising."
2. "In the things I have to do every day, I get enough exercise without doing any sports or athletics."
3. "These fads about physical fitness come and go, and I'm not impressed by this current emphasis on it."
4. "Too much exercising can enlarge the heart, and this is bad when you stop exercising."
5. "Middle-aged and older people don't really need exercise other than walking."
6. "The key to staying fit is not exercise, but to control how much you eat."
7. "People who exercise work up big appetites and then eat too much, making the exercise useless."
8. "The trouble with participating in sport is that I can only get to do it every now and then, and too much physical exertion at one time like that is bad for people."
9. "Too many people, such as joggers and weight lifters, become fanatical about physical fitness, which is not healthy." (109, pp. 25-26)

When 618 people in this survey, were asked to explain why, in a very practical sense, they were not getting enough exercise, their responses were lack of time (47 percent), health reasons (19 percent), family obligations (19 percent), lack of motivation (18 percent), the weather (15 percent), lack of facilities or partners (14 percent), and old age (3 percent). The observation was made that "the primary obstacles to fitness are either self-imposed or caused by lack of information . . . certainly some are offering rationalizations rather than obstacles" (109, p. 51).

Potential fitness swimmers must try to find a balance between the myths (excuses) and the values (benefits) that have been cited so that they can get started in their exercise programs. It takes a minimum of 2–4 weeks and sometimes as long as 6–8 weeks to begin to achieve some of the desirable effects. It's hard work, and it represents a drastic change in some people's life-styles.

It's also a time when you are especially susceptible to other types of influences. You may feel foolish or out of place or all alone, and you may feel that your present skill level is inadequate and will never improve. You may feel intimidated by other swimmers in the pool and that other people are watching you. You may feel that no one else has ever been as inept as you are at this activity. You feel as if your goggles are the only ones which ever have a leak in them, and you feel as if everyone in the building hears you when you choke and cough. You suffer humiliation, embarrassment, and physical distress as a result of your participation, and all the talk about "swimmer's high" leaves you feeling confused and deceived. So you begin to forget your towel or suit or locker combination, and eventually you stop swimming.

There's no single solution to these problems, which happen to people in all types of fitness activities. Many regular fitness swimmers have worked their way through these feelings, and you'll find that they can be tremendously supportive if you'll open up a little and let them help you. Teachers and coaches can help by providing a variety of free swim hours, formal and informal instruction, and plenty of support and encouragement.

External conditions are not nearly as important as your desire to improve your life-style. Self-improvement is difficult without a deep-seated commitment to become the best person that you can become. Remember—you are not the first one to try this, you are not alone in your efforts, and you are not the worst swimmer of all time. Eventually, the positives can far outweigh the negatives in your participation, but you have to give them a chance to happen.

REQUIREMENTS FOR YOUR INVOLVEMENT

The basic requirements for prospective fitness swimmers relate to their knowledge, skill, and attitude. Knowledge mostly consists of your understanding what to do, how to do it, and how to keep it interesting. While some skill is required for participation, you do not have to be a championship swimmer to receive exercise benefits from fitness swimming. Some sort of formal or informal lessons may precede or accompany the start of your fitness swimming program if you can't swim at all or if you can't swim very well. Attitude focuses primarily on your desire to learn, your willingness to challenge yourself physically and mentally, your ability to tolerate some initial discomfort, and your rejection of the many excuses that are used to stay out of the water.

In any pool where people are swimming for fitness, there is a wide range of knowledge, skill, and attitude seen. Some swimmers are tremendously knowledgeable and well-read about swimming and exercise theory; others think hand paddles go on their feet. Some are extremely skillful with competitive strokes and flip turns, and they have a different swimsuit for every day of the week; others swim mostly the crawl stroke, frequently get water up their nose, choke loudly and conspicuously, and try something different only when they think no one is watching. Some are so into swimming that they actually suffer from mental depression if they can't swim eight times a week; the dedication of others reflects less than a lifetime commitment to exercise.

Swimming is a fitness activity which appeals to many different people who have different levels of involvement and interest. The Perrier Study estimates that there are 26 million swimmers in this country (109, p. 6), while another source estimates 60 million adult American swimmers (3, p. 59). But there's always room for one more swimmer in our lane—especially if it's you. Get wet!

REVIEW

Answer as many questions as you can by yourself, then refer to the chapter text or the Index to find the answers to the rest of the questions.

1. Which of the benefits of fitness swimming are most meaningful to you?
2. What are the differences between immediate responses and long-range responses to exercise?
3. Regular exercise will guarantee that you will never have a heart attack. True or False?
4. Regular exercise will guarantee that you will have a long and healthy life. True or False?
5. What is unique about exercising in water?
6. Have you ever experienced any of the psychological benefits of fitness swimming? Which ones? Can you add anything to the descriptions of those benefits in the text?
7. The_____is a heightened sense of well-being while swimming, moving efficiently without great effort and feeling as one with the water.
8. Do you know anyone who is an "exercise addict"? Why do you think they are addicted to exercise?
9. Which of the reasons for not exercising do you relate to most?

CHAPTER TWO
Establishing a Lifetime Program

Fitness swimmers can and should be creative in establishing training programs that fit their own needs, interests, abilities, and goals. This chapter discusses the factors that should be taken into account in the development of individualized lifetime programs.

MEDICAL CHECK

A doctor's approval should be secured before starting a fitness program. "The main objective . . . is to spot heart, lung, and blood vessel problems that could make exercise potentially dangerous" (37, p. 22). For those under 30 years of age, a successful annual checkup is sufficient. For those over 30 the checkup should occur no more than 3 months before the start of exercising.

The use of an exercise stress test before entering an exercise program is a controversial subject. Kenneth Cooper supports this concept:

> A complete cardiac examination not only consists of the blood tests, the medical history, listening to the chest, and blood pressure determination that nearly everyone is familiar with; it also requires that your heart be monitored during rest and exercise with an eletrocardiograph. This monitoring is called a maximal or near-maximal performance exercise electrocardiogram or, in shorter terms, a stress ECG. . . . We have to see how . . . [the heart] performs under stress. When it's functioning at a high rate of speed, it may have difficulties that simply don't show up while you're resting. (36, pp. 13–14)

Medical opinions differ on some fundamental aspects of this type of testing. Some authorities question the predictive value of the exercise stress test in the diagnosis of coronary heart disease (50, 51, 65) while others believe it is of tremendous help in this regard (105). Some physicians are concerned about the accuracy of this test, which may attribute heart disease to subjects who don't have it (false positive results) or may miss conditions that actually exist (false negative results), while others feel that it's the best that can be done short of surgical techniques.

Because medical opinion differs, the safest recommendation is to encourage each prospective fitness swimmer to discuss exercise plans with a physician before beginning a training program. This discussion and evaluation may or may not lead to an exercise stress test, depending on the individual situation. There are some medical conditions that place limitations on vigorous exercise and that require close supervision and monitoring by a physician. So start safely and consult your doctor.

GETTING STARTED

It is important to start vigorous swimming programs gradually in order to let the body condition itself over a period of time and to establish the groundwork for lifetime participation. The long-term effects of inactivity cannot be reversed quickly, and regular, enjoyable, and sustained exercise is required to achieve desirable results.

I began fitness swimming with workouts of only 200–300 yards total length, broken up into shorter distances (low-intensity repeats). The distance was increased by 100 yards every week or two. The National Masters Swim Committee recommends the following approach (94, p. 8):

First 2 weeks: 100 yards each day in four swims of 25 yards each.

2nd–6th week: 200 yards each day in two swims of 100 yards each.

6th–16th week: 400 yards each day in four swims of 100 yards each.

16th–24th week: 600 yards each day in three swims of 200 yards each.

24th–32nd week: 800 yards each day in either four swims of 200 yards each or two swims of 400 yards each.

At 32 weeks: at least 800 yards a day either as eight 100 yards, four 200 yards, two 400 yards, or one 800 yards.

Thereafter: any type of workout you are physically able to perform.

This progression should not be rigidly interpreted. There is some overlap in the weeks to accommodate individual differences. Some people may move through the buildup more slowly or quickly, depending on their starting points. Some of the workouts might be modified slightly within the framework of the total yards listed to provide more variety.

One of the problems in all exercise programs is that people start out with a great burst of enthusiasm and resolution, expend their energy too quickly, and drop out of the program after a relatively short time. Some fitness swimmers are too vigorous and too competitive, working too hard and too soon before leaving the program without achieving any of the long-term benefits. Remember: start slowly, build up gradually, and stay with your program for the rest of your life.

FREQUENCY AND DURATION

Frequency refers to the number of times per week that you exercise, while duration refers to the length of each workout. I have had a good experience swimming three or four times a week, between 800 and 2,000 yards each time (15–50 minutes), taking several breaks throughout the year for school vacations, and doing several other physical activities (weight training, bicycling, basketball) when not swimming. Other authorities have provided a variety of guidelines. Paul Hutinger set an absolute minimum for exercise of 15 minutes a day, 5 days a week, all year long, but highly recommended a program of exercising for 60 minutes a day, 4 or 5 days a week (*71*, p. 27). Ransom Arthur believed that "a challenging mile a day brings most of the benefits" (*15*, p. 47) even though this may not produce maximum competitive performance. The Red Cross has promoted regular and frequent exercise with no weekly minimums, and swimming distances that are multiples of 440 yards (1/4-mile segments) (*2*). Kenneth Cooper recommended aerobic exercise at least three times a week and believed that four times a week is best, and related swimming distances to point values based on oxygen consumption. (*34*, and *37*). Bud Getchell recommended 30 minutes as the ideal length of the "conditioning bout" (*58*, p. 93), while other experts believe that 20 minutes is minimally sufficient.

Vigorous exercise for longer than the recommended durations can contribute to fitness gains, but only up to a certain point. There is a fine line between workouts that promote fitness improvements and workouts that damage the health of the participant. Although tolerance to exercise varies widely among individuals, most authorities agree that, for most people, exercise beyond 1 hour in duration is governed by a law of diminishing returns: the time and effort invested does not compare favorably with the additional fitness benefits that might occur.

Some swimmers use a "cycle training" method (*42*, *129*) in which long, hard workout days are alternated with days on which the workouts are shorter, quicker, and easier. This plan creates variety in the training program, and provides a lighter recovery or recuperation day before the next heavier workout. This method can be used regardless of the number of workout days in the week, and is especially helpful for those who feel the need to be active in the water five, six, or seven times a week. For example, Mondays, Wednesdays, and Fridays can be used for hard workouts, and Tuesdays, Thursdays, and Saturdays can be used for easier workouts.

Never punish yourself—always try to feel good about your workouts and your total training program, even though you may experience some normal discomforts as you work hard for your fitness goals. Positive

11

feelings about your exercise program will help you follow it long enough and regularly enough to reach and maintain the desired long-term fitness benefits.

Factors affecting the frequency and duration of fitness swimming include availability and convenience of the facility, health goals, present level of conditioning, outside demands and pressures, level of energy and enthusiasm, and enjoyment and satisfaction derived from the program. The ideas in this section are guidelines and not absolutes, so challenge yourself, be persistent and realistic, and enjoy yourself.

INTENSITY

In order to create a training effect and receive cardiorespiratory benefit from exercise, fitness swimmers must work at a certain intensity. There are several ways to determine the threshold of exercise intensity required to improve the fitness of the heart, lungs, and blood vessels (the oxygen transporting–processing system). The two methods that will be described here use heart rate as an indicator of exercise intensity. Heart rate is directly related to aerobic capacity (which is a more sophisticated measure of exercise intensity but is less practical for swimmers to use), and individuals usually reach their maximum heart rate and aerobic limits at the same time. Individual characteristics and differences are not usually accounted for in standard formulas, and there are variations in the heart rate responses of different people to vigorous exercise. Fitness swimmers should develop a sensitivity to their personal reactions to their workouts and training programs, and should not be obsessively concerned with some arbitrary standards.

The first method of determining intensity requires that swimmers work out at 70–90 percent of their maximum heart rates. Your maximum heart rate (beats per minute) can be estimated by subtracting your age from 220. For example:

	220 (standard)			
	-31			
(maximum heart rate)	189	$\times$	.70 =	132 beats per minute during exercise
(maximum heart rate)	189	$\times$	.90 =	170 beats per minute during exercise

This fitness swimmer should try to swim at a speed or pace that will maintain the heart rate between 130 and 170 beats per minute during a continuous swim or during repeat swims.

The second method of determining intensity is known as the Karvonen Formula (58, p. 86) and is expressed as follows:

$$\text{training heart rate} = \text{resting heart rate} + 60\% \left(\text{maximum heart rate} - \text{resting heart rate} \right)$$

Note: Resting heart rate is taken as the individual stands quietly, and maximum heart rate is again computed as 220 minus your age.

Using the example of a 31-year-old swimmer,

$$
\begin{aligned}
\text{training heart rate} \quad &= 75 + .60\,(189 - 75) \\
&= 75 + .60\,(114) \\
&= 75 + 68 \\
&= 143 \text{ beats per minute}
\end{aligned}
$$

This fitness swimmer should try to swim at a speed or pace that will maintain the heart rate at or above 140 beats per minute during a continuous swim or during repeat swims.

Getchell noted that the Karvonen Formula represented a *minimum* value, and he established "an increase in heart rate equal to 75 percent of the difference between resting and maximal heart rates as a safe and reasonable intensity for most participants." (58, p. 86). When applied to the previous example, we get the following calculation:

$$
\begin{aligned}
\text{training heart rate} \quad &= 75 + .75(189 - 75) \\
&= 75 + .75(114) \\
&= 75 + 85.5 \\
&= 160.5 \text{ beats per minute}
\end{aligned}
$$

This fitness swimmer should try to swim at a speed or pace that will maintain the heart rate at or above 160 beats per minute during a continous swim or during repeat swims.

Another complicating factor in the use of heart rate formulas for fitness swimmers is the fact your maximum heart rate and your exercising heart rate each tend to be about 10 beats slower while swimming than for comparable exertion on land (45, 67, 95). You may want to adjust the recommended minimum exercising heart rates down 10 beats to reflect this phenomenon, which is caused mostly by the swimmer's horizontal position in the water. For the average fitness swimmer, this may mean a reduction in the lower and upper limits of the range of their target heart rates during exercise, and emphasizes the need to use common sense in applying standardized formulas to personal situations. For cross-over swimmers (those who also run or cycle), this phenomenon can be discouraging unless they understand why they have a slightly lower exercising heart rate while swimming.

Fitness swimmers can learn to count their own heart rates throughout their exercise (between repeat sets) and at the end of their workouts to make sure they have worked hard enough to benefit from their activity. By using a pace clock or a secondhand on a watch, the heart rate can be counted for a certain time period and then multiplied by a standard to convert that number to the heart rate in beats per minute. You can count for 6 seconds and multipy by 10, or count for 15 seconds and multiply by 4, or count for 10 seconds and multiply by 6. Many people prefer the first method listed because of its mathematical ease—simply put a zero on the end of whatever number the 6-second count is, and you have your heart rate in beats per minute.

Usually, the heart rate is taken at the carotid artery, the pulse of which can be felt at the side of the throat. Extremely light pressure should be used by the fingertips, just enough to pick up and count the pulse but not enough to distort the wall of this artery in any way (19). The heart rate should be counted *immediately* when the individual stops swimming. Even a brief delay can reduce the count as the heart begins its return to a normal state following the stopping of the exercise.

There are electronic devices that can be used to check your heart rate. These devices (available in water-resistant models) are activated by grasping the sensitized ends with your hands, completing a circuit which converts your heart rate into a digital display. Some devices use an "average" mode of display, while others present the heart rate in the "beat-to-beat" mode (25). It may be possible to mount the device near poolside on a starting block using special clamps, enabling fitness swimmers to reach up and check their heart rates frequently during their workouts. If available, these devices should be used because of their convenience and high accuracy. However, fitness swimmers should learn to count their heart rates themselves, since they may not always have access to this type of sophisticated device.

The basic problem in exercise intensity is to determine a level of exercise that will lead to fitness benefits and improvements without exhausting you. Most of the formulas translate into practical heart rate values during exercise as follows: 140–180 beats per minute for young adults or well-conditioned participants, and 120–160 beats per minute for older people or unconditioned participants. Intensity levels may change in different workouts or within the same workout, and fitness swimmers should remember that these heart rate guidelines represent averages to maintain in their workouts and total training programs (58, p. 94).

DIET AND WEIGHT CONTROL

Many swimmers participate in fitness swimming with the hope of losing weight. A vigorous program of fitness swimming can provide the increased level of activity that is an essential part of most weight control programs, but this may not be enough to produce weight loss by itself. Weight loss also depends on decreasing your intake of calories. You have to swim very far to burn up a substantial amount of calories, and those calories that are burned up can be replaced quickly and easily in your daily food intake.

There are hundreds of diet books available, and all of them have their staunch advocates and followers. Unfortunately, many of them present totally conflicting ideas and advice. Because people are different and have different metabolisms, different diets will work well for different people. Most important is to have self-discipline, willpower, and common sense about food intake. Those who are not familiar with elements of sound nutrition should consult a physician or dietician for professional advice to ensure a balanced diet. Weight loss should be gradual, perhaps 1–2 pounds per week for most people. It is important to avoid the "yo-yo effect" in which you follow a steady cycle of being on a diet/losing weight alternated with being off the diet/regaining the weight. Remember that you are not likely to change your total personality, temperament, and body type just by reorganizing your eating habits.

There is no special food or special diet plan that could be fairly presented as being ideal for swimming. Some swimmers have strong food preferences but psychological factors may be involved (if you *believe* something will help you perform better, you may perform better). There is no magical food that should be eaten the night before a big workout or race—despite the true stories of the Egyptian swimmers who ate great quantities of eggs and chickens in their highly successful attempts at swimming the English Channel and the young woman who ate three chocolate-chip cookies during her record-setting swim across the Channel. The traditional advice applies here: use common sense, eat less in a balanced diet, and exercise more.

PLANNING

Fitness swimmers should plan their workouts in advance, and then carry them out as planned. The advance planning can create a sense of anticipation and enthusiasm, and the follow-through to completion can create a sense of accomplishment. This planning may be from day to day, on a weekly basis, or for several weeks in the future in terms of training goals and ideas. You should rarely change a workout in the middle of doing it—this makes your workout subject to whim and transient feelings of fatigue. Challenge yourself—finish what you've set out to do.

KEEPING A DIARY

Some very serious swimmers keep records or diaries of their daily programs. It's a way for them to summarize an important part of their life. Contents include workouts, competitive and repeat times, special variations in the workout, body weight, health problems, total distances, stroke problems and corrections, future goals, new ideas, subjective feelings about the workout, and personal items. This daily writing makes the swimmers more thoughtful, focusing their mental energies on their training program. Comparing your present status with what you have done in the past can be highly rewarding and motivating, but we usually can't rely on memory. So a written record is necessary for such comparisons.

VARIETY

The opportunities for variety in the training program are limitless, and truly qualify this activity as one that can be done for a whole lifetime of healthful enjoyment. Follow the advice given here and you will never have to dread doing the same old thing over and over again.

Mix it up—never do the same workout twice in a row or even more than once a week. Use different strokes for different parts of your workout. Do some medley swimming, rotating 25, 50, or 100 yards with different strokes in a long swim. Do some interval training, and do some long continuous swims (see Chapter 7). If the facility permits, swim over the short course (25 yards) at times and over the long course (50 meters) at other times. Skip a day occasionally, and sometimes do two workouts in a day. Try an early morning swim with a local team (5:30 or 6:30 A.M. will really wake you up), or swim late in the evening under the stars. Do some pulling, kicking, and swimming as part of your workout, and occasionally do a whole workout of just pulling, just kicking, or just swimming. Use a pull buoy to practice your hand action with or without hand paddles. Use a kickboard to practice your foot action with or without swim fins. Do your kicking without a kickboard. Use the pace clock to help you push a workout hard. Do a whole workout with no reference to your times—don't even look at the pace clock. Jog in the water. Do some long swims in open water if you're near a beach (follow sensible safety precautions). Take a break from swimming to do some other lifetime physical activities, or to do nothing at all if you want.

Remember, a principal psychological benefit of exercise is diversity in your life, a pleasant change of pace in your daily routine. Don't grind out the same old swim every day.

BREAKS IN TRAINING

Don't feel pressured into swimming all year, everyday, if you feel that you need a break in training. For example, I swim about 40 weeks a year, which corresponds to the time school is in session, with school vacations reserved for other activities or no exercise at all. Some swimmers alternate periods of high intensity and low intensity in their training programs, recognizing how difficult it is to push extremely hard all the time. Psychologically, short training breaks help to alleviate the staleness, boredom, and monotony that can set in when you do the same thing day in and day out. Other vigorous aerobic activities, and sufficient rest and relaxation, should play important roles for those whose goal is fitness for life. When you return to fitness swimming after a break, remember to start in slowly and build back up to your own level of exercise gradually.

SUMMARY

The phrase "exercise prescription" is a way of summarizing some of the most essential elements in planning your training program (127, p. 48). For many fitness swimmers, the prescription would read as follows:

Type of exercise—fitness swimming.

Frequency—three or four times a week, or every other day over a 2-week cycle.

Intensity—target heart rate of at least 140 beats per minute, adjusted according to age and the appropriate formulas.

Duration—main part of workout, excluding brief warm-up and warm-down, to take approximately 30 minutes.

Pattern—continuous swimming (no rests) and/or interval swimming (alternate swimming and resting; see Chapter 7).

Variety—deliberate and continual changes in the combinations of different distances and strokes, the use of different pieces of equipment, and the distribution of pulling, kicking, and swimming components in different workouts.

Lifetime commitment—long-term involvement with aerobic exercise.

REVIEW

Answer as many questions as you can by yourself, then refer to the chapter text or the Index to find the answers to the rest of the questions.

1. Have you secured medical clearance before starting your exercise program?
2. What is meant by a gradual start in your exercise program?
3. _____refers to the number of times per week that you exercise.
4. The alternation of hard workout days with easier workout days is called_____.

5. How long you exercise is called _____.

6. How hard you exercise is called _____.

7. How is your heart rate related to exercise intensity?

8. Calculate your target heart rate for exercising, first, according to the Karvonen formula and, second, according to the Karvonen formula as revised by Getchell.

9. Why is your heart rate lower while swimming than for comparable exertion on land?

10. How could you add more variety into your workouts?

11. Discuss the relative importance of exercise or diet in weight loss and control?

12. What is meant by an exercise prescription?

CHAPTER THREE
Breathing Exercises

Aerobic exercise (exercise that uses oxygen) depends on continual air exchange (inhalation and exhalation), even during heavy exertion. Inadequate breathing has always been a limiting factor in participation in swimming, in that swimmers who don't breathe easily while doing various strokes and skills usually tend to avoid the activity. You will become extremely fatigued or uncomfortable if you are gasping for air, inhaling water, or holding your breath while you swim. Unfortunately, many swimming instructors have not put adequate emphasis on breathing exercises in their teaching methods.

Fitness swimmers should work on their breathing patterns so that they can sustain their exercise long enough to gain fitness benefits from it. The procedures described in this chapter form a rough progression for learning alternate side breathing (breathing to either side in the crawl stroke). They may be practiced as part of a workout or in special sessions devoted to breathing patterns. Practice these procedures frequently at the beginning of your exercise program to reach the goal of full, continual air exchange during different strokes and skills. Later, use parts of this progression in your workouts as a periodic check on your breathing capacities. Continual air exchange is a key to fitness swimming, and with practice you'll soon feel comfortable breathing as you swim.

BOBBING

Bobbing is the basic breathing exercise while in the water. The slow, steady, rhythmic breathing pattern of bobbing is best learned in water that is about shoulder deep. While standing on the bottom of the pool, bend the knees so that the head submerges completely, then stand up again so that the mouth is above the surface. These down-and-up movements are repeated over and over again with a continuous breathing pattern: breathe in primarily through the mouth whenever the face is above the water, and breathe out primarily through the nose (some from the mouth) whenever the face is under the water (both on the descent and on the ascent). Figure 3–1 illustrates this pattern.

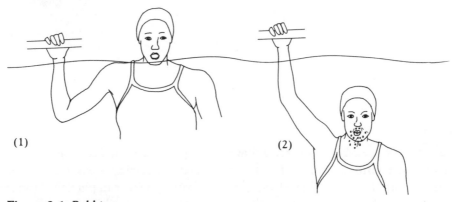

Figure 3-1. Bobbing.

1. *Take a deep breath in.*
2. *Submerge and exhale. Keep exhaling as you return to the surface.*

It is extremely important to maintain full, steady, continuous exhalation through the nose on the way down and on the way up. This means that you are *not* gasping for air, *not* getting water up your nose, and *not* holding your breath between inhalations. When you do breathe, all you need to do is to breathe in, rather than trying to exhale and inhale quickly above the water surface in a relatively short period of time. Some air will also be released through the mouth when you are exercising hard in the water, but the primary emphasis is on blowing air out steadily through the nose. In time, you will become accustomed to breathing with water running down over the hair, eyes, nose and mouth as your head comes up above the surface of the water. Keep the head still, don't shake it around, or the bobbing rhythm will be lost.

Once you are comfortable doing the basic exercise in shoulder-deep water, it's time to practice bobbing in water just over the head in depth. To begin the initial descent in deeper water, the head, shoulders, and upper part of the chest should be lifted above the surface of the water by pushing downward with the arms and legs. With the legs together and the arms by the sides, the weight of these body parts above the water will force you underwater in a vertical descent. The feet may be separated as you touch the bottom of the pool. After bending the knees slightly, push off the bottom to begin the ascent to the surface. As you reach the surface, the head should come up only high enough to breathe in through the mouth before submerging again. These down-and-up movements are repeated rhythmically over and over again in coordination with the continous breathing pattern described previously (in primarily through the mouth, out primarily through the nose underwater).

As you develop more skill and feel even more comfortable, a few other variations can be introduced. Normally, bobbing is done in a stationary position, but travel bobbing may be done by leaning forward slightly during each push from the bottom, ascending to the surface each time at a slight angle. Ultimately, try to perform the skill in even deeper water than just over the head. A bobbing depth of 8–10 feet is a worthwhile goal for fitness swimmers. You might also use bobbing for a minute or two as a way of finishing a workout, simply bobbing until your breathing has returned to a more normal state. This is a relaxing way to conclude a workout, and a good test of breathing capacities.

BENEFITS OF ALTERNATE SIDE BREATHING

The ability to breathe to both sides in crawl stroke (alternate side breathing) provides the fitness swimmer with several benefits:

1. It tends to make the hand and arm strokes equal on both sides. Usually, the arm on the regular breathing side tends to be stronger and more propulsive. This is balanced with alternate side breathing.
2. There is often considerable tension in the shoulder of the arm on the non-breathing side, especially during the recovery (the return of the arm over the surface), because it usually rides a little lower in the water than the other shoulder. This tension can be reduced and relieved by breathing to opposite sides alternately, making the shoulder less susceptible to pain and injury.
3. Alternate side breathing is an expression of breath control ability and comfort. Fitness swimmers who can do this will be "in charge" of their own breathing patterns rather than always feeling as if they are controlled by their desperate need for air. They will be able to sustain distance swims and repeat swims with the full, continual air exchange that is essential for attaining aerobic exercise benefits.

FLUTTER KICKING AND BREATHING

Flutter kicking with breathing (Figure 3-2) is first learned against the wall of the swimming pool. While lying on the front, grasp the pool gutter with the hands and support the feet and legs with a slow, easy flutter kick. Your elbows may bend very slightly to help maintain body position and to facilitate breathing to the side. Some beginners modify this by keeping their feet on the bottom of the pool as they grasp the wall, and this enables them to keep their balance better and to focus strictly on the breathing pattern.

In this position, five basic breathing patterns can be emphasized:

● Right side only: Breathe to the right side, turn the face down and

21

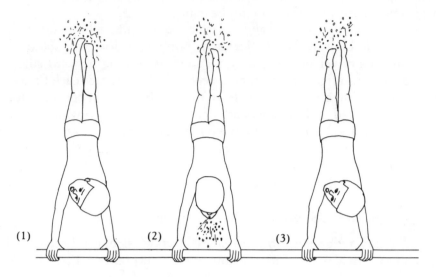

Figure 3-2. Flutter Kicking and Side Breathing

1. *Turn face to the side and breathe in.*
2. *Turn face down and exhale.*
3. *Turn face to the side and breathe in again.*

exhale (primarily through the nose), breathe to the right side, turn the face down and exhale, etc.

- Left side only: Breathe to the left side, turn the face down and exhale, breathe to the left side, turn the face down and exhale, etc.
- Alternate side breathing (1 to the right and 1 to the left): Breathe to the right side, turn the face down and exhale, breathe to the left side, turn the face down and exhale, breathe to the right side, etc.
- Alternate side breathing (2 to the right and 2 to the left): Breathe twice consecutively to the right side, then switch over and breathe twice consecutively to the left side, etc. Exhale when your face is down.
- Alternate side breathing (3 to the right and 3 to the left): Breathe three times consecutively to the right, then switch over and breathe three times consecutively to the left, etc. Exhale when your face is down.

Once the breathing pattern has been mastered against the wall, forward movement can be added by doing the same breathing drills with a kickboard. Instead of the wall, the board is held by the hands on its sides, about one-quarter to one-third of the way up from the base or bottom, with the elbows straight or very slightly bent, and with the thumbs on top. The front edge of the board may ride up a little bit, as the board is held

22

nearly flat on the surface of the water. Kick slowly, work on the five different breathing patterns, and concentrate on full inhalation through the mouth and steady exhalation underwater primarily through the nose. Fitness swimmers whose crawl stroke kicks are not well developed should do these drills with swim fins on their feet. This will change their focus of attention from a weak kick to concentration on effective breathing patterns.

Whether practicing these drills against the wall or with a kickboard, beginners tend to make the common mistake of lifting the head and looking forward before turning the head to the side to inhale through the mouth. You need to feel the surface of the water at or slightly above the hairline, and to breathe only to the side. Try to keep the ear opposite the breathing side in the water as you turn to breathe. For example, if you breathe to the right, keep your left ear in the water. The shoulders should turn along with the head and neck during the side breathing, and the body should not be held in a flat position except when the face is down for exhaling into the water.

STANDING AND BREATHING

Breathing patterns may be learned while in a stationary position in water that is about waist-deep or chest-deep (Figure 3-3). You'll need to brace yourself with your hands on the top of the pool wall, your legs bent slightly, and your feet on the bottom of the pool. If you're breathing to the left, get your right foot forward; if you're breathing to the right, get your left foot forward; if you're doing an alternating pattern, keep your feet even. Bend forward to simulate a crawl stroke position in the water, and move your hands in a stroking pattern slowly enough so that you don't pull yourself out of that braced, stationary position.

In all of the five breathing patterns, concentrate on full exhalation underwater before breathing to the side. When the head turns to breathe, all you should need to do is to inhale through the mouth. Right-sided breathing is begun when the right hand and arm reach the level of the right shoulder in the underwater pull (the stroking pattern of the hand and arm through the water). Breathing to that side can be completed as the underwater pull is finished. Then, the face can be turned back down as the hand and arm move over the surface in the recovery. Left-sided breathing is done in similar fashion to that side.

If you wait until your hand is back by your hip or leg before turning your head to breathe, your breathing can be described as "too late." If your head is turning to the side to breathe and your arm is starting to recover over the water at the same time, usually the arm carries some water on it which is thrown in your face; this distracts beginners and makes them very uncomfortable in their initial breathing efforts. If you breathe as the hand and arm is pulling back underwater, all of the movements of the hand,

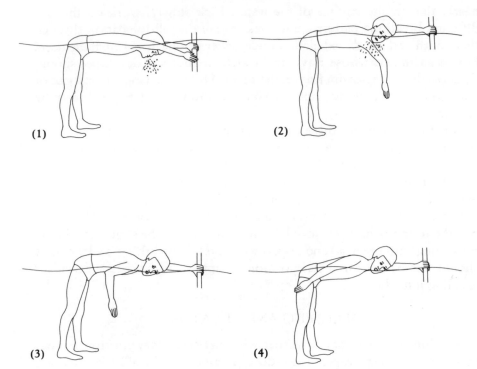

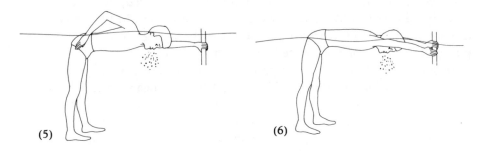

Figure 3-3. Standing and Side Breathing.

1. *Exhale with face down.*
2. *Turn head to the side as you finish exhaling.*
3. *With head turned to the side (not lifted up), breathe in.*
4. *Finish breathing in as arm is pulled back.*
5. *Turn face down and exhale, continuing to exhale as hand and arm move over the surface in the recovery.*
6. *Keep exhaling slowly. Stroke once with left arm, then repeat the arm stroke and breathing pattern to the right side.*

arm, shoulders, head, and neck will begin to fit together smoothly in a coordinated breathing pattern.

Practicing various breathing patterns while in a standing, stationary position is extremely important for many beginning fitness swimmers who experience breathing difficulties. In time, that same relaxed feeling that you can get as you breathe in a standing position can actually transfer into your stroke as you move through the water. Use this stage as a quick review if you have occasional problems with your breathing after your initial learning process.

PULLING AND BREATHING

Breathing patterns may be learned while practicing only the hand and arm action of the crawl stroke (pulling). A pull buoy (a flotation-type device) is held between the legs and above the knees (Figure 3-4). Buoyancy is greatly improved, no kicking is necessary, and you can focus on your new and effective breathing patterns. You should turn to either side just enough to breathe in a small trough formed by your cheek and open mouth, by the turning of the head and shoulders at the same time, and by the effect of your forward momentum through the water.

With the pull buoy, and working *slowly* at one-half to three-quarter speed, practice breathing only to the right side every stroke in crawl stroke. You should also practice breathing every stroke only to the left side. Next, practice alternate side breathing for crawl stroke, breathing every third stroke to opposite sides. Many beginners make the mistake of trying to breathe every stroke to opposite sides, and this discourages them because they can't turn fast enough to keep up. In a sense, you "skip a stroke" to create a pattern that is manageable by breathing every other stroke or every third stroke to opposite sides. Also, practice breathing 2 to the right and 2 to the left, and 3 to the right and 3 to the left.

CRAWL STROKE AND BREATHING

The five breathing patterns should be practiced while swimming the crawl stroke without the pull buoy. Most swimmers have a "weak side" in their breathing at the beginning. To develop the weak side, make it a habit to breathe to that side out of every turn and push-off for one or two strokes before continuing with the breathing pattern you have chosen for the rest of the length. If this is done conscientiously, it won't be long until both breathing sides are equal, or at least more equal. You should constantly add variety to your workouts by trying different breathing patterns for the crawl stroke.

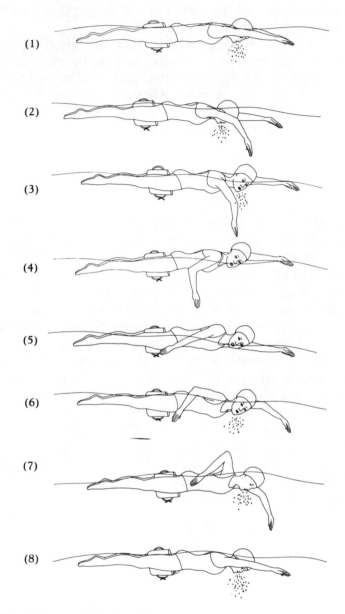

(1)

(2)

(3)

(4)

(5)

(6)

(7)

(8)

Figure 3-4. Pulling and Side Breathing.

1. *With pull buoy held above knees, exhale with face down.*
2. *Begin right arm stroke.*
3. *Turn head to the side, still exhaling.*
4. *With head turned to the side (not lifted up), breathe in.*
5. *Finish breathing in as arm is pulled back.*
6. *Turn face down and exhale as you begin left arm stroke.*
7. *Keep exhaling slowly into the water.*
8. *Left arm begins its recovery as you repeat right arm stroke and right side breathing pattern.*

26

ONE-ARM SWIMMING AND BREATHING

One-arm swimming for crawl stroke may be done with or without a pull buoy. To use the right arm, hold the left hand and arm straight out in front of the left shoulder. While stroking only with the right hand and arm, breathe every stroke to the right side only. To use the left arm, hold the right arm in front of the right shoulder, stroke only with the left arm, and breathe only to the left every stroke. This drill usually alternates lengths of right arm only and left arm only, and strengthens both the arm pull and the breathing pattern to that side.

OTHER STROKES

The breathing exercises described in this chapter, although geared toward the crawl stroke, will ultimately contribute to success and comfort in breathing in the other strokes as well. Specific breathing patterns for the different strokes will be included in Chapter 5. The final goal is to be able to breathe fully and comfortably without even thinking about it while you swim.

REVIEW

Rate yourself as honestly and accurately as you can on the following checklist of in-the-water skills

SKILL	IMPROVE-MENT NEEDED	ADE-QUATE	GOOD
bobbing	_____	_____	_____
flutter kicking and side breathing			
against the wall	_____	_____	_____
on a kickboard	_____	_____	_____
standing and side breathing	_____	_____	_____
pulling and side breathing	_____	_____	_____
crawl—right side only	_____	_____	_____
crawl—left side only	_____	_____	_____
crawl—1 to right and 1 to left	_____	_____	_____
crawl—2 to right and 2 to left	_____	_____	_____
crawl—3 to right and 3 to left	_____	_____	_____
one-arm swimming and side breathing			
right side	_____	_____	_____
left side	_____	_____	_____

Continue to work in the pool on improving your weaknesses. Set some long-term goals for skill improvement and tailor your fitness swimming workouts to help you reach those goals. Use this checklist once or twice a year to chart your progress.

CHAPTER FOUR
Use of Equipment

Y ou should become familiar with the equipment that is available for use in your exercise programs. This equipment provides comfort, challenge, and/or variety. With the exception of personal items, it should be supplied by the management of the pool facility, either left out in storage bins for general use or checked out and back in again through an equipment room.

SWIMSUIT AND CAP

A swimsuit can be purchased at most department or sporting goods stores. Many regular swimmers use nylon suits because they dry out faster between uses. Female fitness swimmers seem more comfortable in one-piece suits, although two-piece suits can be worn. Male fitness swimmers seem more comfortable in brief-style trunks, although boxer-style trunks can be worn if they don't cause leg chafing or irritation. Swimsuits should be rinsed occasionally in fresh water to wash out the pool chemicals. Several suits may be rotated to ensure complete drying between uses.

Lightweight rubber bathing caps are sometimes used by either men or women to prevent contact with the chlorinated water, but those who do not wear caps simply wash their hair right after they swim to rinse out any pool chemicals. Some pools require that people with long hair wear bathing caps, since it is thought that long hair can clog drains, pipes, and the "hair-catcher" filter. Also, the use of a cap may create a beneficial streamlining effect in competition.

GOGGLES

The use of swim goggles gives you two significant benefits: (1) when properly adjusted and fitted, the goggles will prevent the direct continual contact with pool water that may lead to eye irritation; and (2) the air space created between the goggles and each eyeball permits clear vision underwater. A standard pair of goggles consists of two plastic lenses with

29

soft rims or foam-type molding around the inside edges, an elastic strap or headband, and an adjustable nosepiece (Figure 4–1). The lenses may be clear or tinted in a variety of colors, and may be shaped to permit several visual fields, from straight ahead to wide-angle peripheral vision. Goggles can be purchased with your own prescription lenses in them, and this is a tremendous advantage to swimmers who have poor eyesight. The strap may be thin or wide, made of rubber or cloth-covered elastic, and secured by small locking devices on each side. Be sure to write your name on the strap, since goggles are frequently "lost."

There will be an initial break-in period with a new pair of goggles requiring constant adjustment. After a few workouts, only occasional readjustments will have to be made to keep your goggles fitting well. Rarely, some type or brand of goggle might not fit well with your eye sockets no matter how many adjustments you make. Trade with someone else or buy a new pair with a different style to get the proper fit.

Because of temperature differences between your face and the water, swim goggles will fog up unless you take preventive measures: before you put your goggles on, rub saliva onto the inside of the lenses and then rinse them out and dump the contents into the pool gutter or drains. Defogging solutions are also available at scuba diving shops and may be used in place of your own saliva. Usually, one defogging will last for your whole workout, although you might have to repeat the process if the water is cold.

Occasionally rinse your goggles in fresh water. New headbands can be purchased at most fabric or sewing stores and from swimming supply shops. Keep the spare parts from older broken goggles, and you'll be able to perform minor repairs easily.

You can learn to do all swimming strokes, turns, and related skills better while wearing goggles. You can even do dive starts with your goggles on if you tighten them up and keep your head down on entry before looking forward and getting back up to the surface. Many Masters swimmers use their goggles during competition, and this improved vision can lead to improved times once you become comfortable with the dive entry.

Goggles are relatively inexpensive and their benefits far outweigh the few small inconveniences. Anyone who is serious about fitness swimming (from beginner to advanced levels) should use them.

PULL BUOY

Pull buoys, which can be used to practice a variety of pulling movements, are made of nonabsorbent buoyant materials and are available in several sizes. The two cylinders of the pull buoy are bound together by an adjustable rope or rubber tubing, or may be molded into a one-piece buoy (Figure 4-1).

Figure 4-1. Standard equipment: (*1*) goggles, (*2*) pull buoy, (*3*) kickboard, (*4*) hand paddles, (*5*) fins.

The pull buoy is held between the legs and above the knees, so no kicking is necessary when using the device. When held properly, the pull buoy permits the practice of all the strokes, turns, and push-offs, and very closely duplicates the body position in swimming. When using the pull buoy, you can focus all your energy and concentration on the hand and arm actions of different strokes (pulling).

KICKBOARD

Kickboards (Figure 4-1), which can be used to practice a variety of kicking movements, are made of different kinds of nonabsorbent buoyant materials, in different thicknesses, shapes, sizes, and colors. When kicking on the front, you should hold the board about one-quarter or one-third of the way up from the base end. Hold the board along its sides with your thumbs on top and fingers underneath. Keep your elbows straight or nearly so, and keep your shoulders at or just beneath the surface of the water. The board should ride nearly flat on the surface of the water while kicking. If you hold the board along its top edge and ride up on top of the board, you may cause the feet to drop too low in the water (thereby weakening the kick) and you may experience some low back pain due to the excessive arching of the back. When kicking on the back, you can hold the board over your stomach with your hands on each side of the board, or you may simply hold the board with one hand off to the side of your body.

31

Occasionally, you should practice kicking without using a kickboard. While kicking on the front without a kickboard, kick as usual with the hands stretched out in front of the shoulders, moving the hands a little each time that you breathe to the front. While kicking on the back without a kickboard, kick as usual with the hands held by your sides. If you kick well on your back and feel very comfortable, try holding your hands stretched out over your head for an additional challenge.

HAND PADDLES

Hand paddles come in different sizes, shapes, and colors, and add another dimension to pulling. The paddles are held against the hands by adjustable straps or rubber tubing (Figure 4–1). The paddles may be made with a flat plastic surface, or may be contoured on one side to fit into the palm of the hand.

The large surface areas of the paddles create greater force application against the water during the hand and arm action, and the swimmer can feel greater resistance against the hand during the underwater stroke. There may be some strength-building aspects related to the use of hand paddles. If you are concentrating on technique, the use of hand paddles can alter and improve sensory perception, revealing mistakes in the pitch and path of the hands both underwater and over the surface. This can lead to stroke corrections.

Hand paddles should be used occasionally by all fitness swimmers. They provide a good comparison with the normal hand position used in the various strokes and the normal water pressure felt by the hand. Another interesting comparison is to swim with the hands clenched ("fist swimming"), and to feel the effect of the loss of the propulsive surfaces of the hands and palms against the water. During fist swimming, attention can be focused particularly on the propulsive surfaces of the forearms and the strong movements of the shoulder joints in the pulling action.

Safety should be emphasized because hand paddles can become dangerous weapons in a crowded lane. Serious injuries can result from striking another swimmer with the paddles. To avoid injury, swim straight, space yourselves in the lanes, and be alert to what's around you at all times.

SWIM FINS

Swim fins add a new aspect to variety in your training program, make kicking fun for many swimmers, and give your legs a good workout. Don't overuse them, but add them to your program for these extra benefits. Swim fins alter and improve the kicker's sensory perception ("feel" of the foot and leg actions), and the large surface areas of the fins create greater force application which leads to increased speed in the water. Mistakes in the movement patterns of the different kicks can be revealed and corrected when using swim fins.

Shoe-type fins come in different sizes (small, medium, medium-large, and large) and enclose the entire foot when they are worn. Strap-type fins also come in different sizes and are held to the foot by means of an adjustable strap around the heel. (Figure 4-1 shows both types of fin.) A comfortable fit is necesary, and some swimmers use oversize fins with a pair of heavy socks to ensure a good fit and to prevent chafing.

When you are finished using your fins, empty any water that may have collected in them back into the pool. Store the fins upside down on top of each other so they will drain and dry out between use. Periodically, rinse the fins in fresh water.

You can fin kick with or without a kickboard, on the surface or underwater, and on your front, back, or side. Although the fins do not work for breaststroke kick or elementary backstroke kick, they can be used effectively for the butterfly kick (dolphin kick), backstroke kick (flutter kick on the back), crawl stroke kick (flutter kick on the front), and sidestroke kick (scissors kick). You can also combine fin kicking with the hand action to swim any of these strokes in proper coordination. Because the fins tend to "stick" to the pool wall, you must ease up a little on the push-offs after you turn, leaving the wall without a vigorous, explosive push.

DRAG DEVICES

There are several devices that you can use to create resistance to progress through the water (Figure 4-2). One of these devices is known as a drag board or "pull board" (113, p. 108) and is available in four sizes (small, medium, large, and collegiate). This flat, buoyant board has two holes into which you slide your ankles. When you assume a swimming position, the surface of the board becomes vertical in the water, creating a drag effect. You'll probably prefer to use this device in combination with a pull buoy, but it can be used by itself. The drag board works especially well for crawl stroke but can also be used for the other strokes.

Another device is known as a drag suit (39), which is really a refinement of an old concept of swimming hard while wearing several swimming suits, or a tee shirt and gym shorts, or a sweatsuit. This device has large exterior pockets which expand and fill with water as you swim to create a drag effect. The best drag suits do not alter normal body position in the water, and permit you to swim any stroke. Either the drag board or the drag suit may be used for all or part of a fitness workout.

A third device, a stretching tether, can be constructed of surgical tubing (3/8 inch outer diameter and 3/16 inch inner diameter with 18–20 feet of tubing works well in a 25-yard pool). One end of the tubing is tied to a belt which goes around the swimmer's waist, and the other end forms a loop to

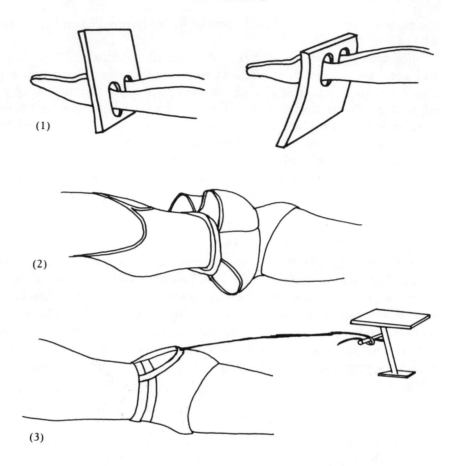

Figure 4-2. Drag devices: *(1)* drag board, *(2)* drag suit, *(3)* stretching tether.

secure the tether to a starting block. The swimmer swims out as far as possible against the increasing resistance of the stretching tether, turns, and then returns very quickly with an assist from the strongly contracting elastic tubing.

In the first length, the further the swimmer goes the harder it becomes to go any further against the stretch of the tether. In the second length, the swimmer uses the principle of "forced fast movement" *(55, and 111)* in which the swimmer sprints faster than normally possible while assisted by the pull of the tether. Experiment with the position of the junction of the belt and tubing to find a position (front, back, side) that is comfortable for you. If you are unable to stretch the tubing completely across the pool, you should swim hard and hold your maximum stretch position for at least 10 seconds before turning and returning very fast. An example of a workout set on a stretching tether is: sprint-5 × 50 crawl; or, distance-continuous 250; or, stroke - 5 × 50 (1 stroke, 1 crawl, 1 stroke, 1 crawl, 1 stroke).

Safety precautions with the stretching tether include periodic inspection of the surgical tubing; replacement of frayed tubing; and never standing directly in line with the stretched tubing.

Drag devices introduce more variety into your training program. You are forced to work harder against the increased resistance (drag) to your movement, and there will be some conditioning and strengthening benefits because of this. A curious sensory effect occurs when the devices are removed because the swimmer feels smoother and faster in the water. You will feel in touch with the flow of the water over your skin as you swim (an unusual sensitivity to speed and acceleration), which is a sensation we normally don't perceive in our regular swims.

WEIGHTED DEVICES

Fitness swimmers can use weighted devices (Figure 4-3) in several different ways as they swim in the water. Wrist weights (128) are ¼ – ½ pound weights which strap around the wrist with Velcro fasteners. The smaller model is adjustable from 1 to 4 ounces, and both can also be used on the swimmer's ankles during kicking. Two main effects are noted:

1. Sensation: The light added weight makes the swimmer more aware of the hand and arm stroke, and this awareness can help improve and refine technique. The swimmer "feels the stroke" better, especially in terms of the rhythm, timing, and speed of the hands. This concept is summarized by the word "isokinesthetics" (123) which means excercising through a full range of movement against a constant weight with special attention to the perception of the position and movements of body parts.

2. Overload: Although the wrist-weights are relatively light, they can be moved literally thousands of times in a normal workout; this low-weight, high-repetition program promotes the development of the factor of muscular endurance.

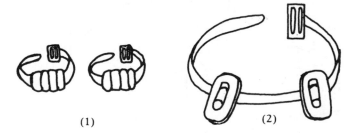

(1)   (2)

Figure 4-3. Weighted devices: (1) wrist-weights and (2) scuba weight belt.

Fitness swimmers can add some dead weight to themselves by strapping on a scuba weight belt. Between 4 and 10 pounds is sufficient to make the swimmer work harder against a constant extra load. If strapped around the waist with the weights on the back above the hips, the belt will not interfere in any way with stroke execution. One or two pull buoys should also be used to counterbalance the heavy negative buoyancy and to enable the swimmer to maintain proper technique with the hands and arms. Strap the weight belt around one or two kickboards to practice kicking against greater resistance. Using the scuba weight belt can also be a good illustration to an overweight swimmer of how much influence extra weight can have on your speed and efficiency in the water.

PACE CLOCK

A pace clock is used to time the speed of your distance or repeat swims, the length of your rest periods, and the brief period in which you count your heart rate. One type of pace clock is large and flat (42 inches wide and 41 inches high) and may be mounted on the wall or on a rolling stand (Figure 4-4). Two motor-driven clock hands (the faster hand on a minute sweep and the slower hand on an hour sweep) move continuously on a clock face marked from 0 to 60. The other type of pace clock is electronic, digital, and programmable (Figure 4-4). A manual setting will run this pace clock from 0 to 99:59, and then start the timing cycle over again. An automatic setting can be used for interval training, in which a preset time cycle is repeated over and over again for a preset number of repetitions. Regardless of the type of clock used, the power source used should be grounded and the power cords should be kept out of puddles of water and up off the wet pool deck.

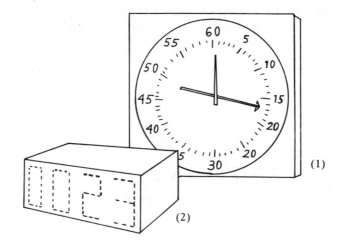

Figure 4-4. Pace clocks: (1) manual (2) digital.

It will take a while for beginning fitness swimmers to feel comfortable using a pace clock. You need to practice reading the clock, refer to it frequently as you exercise, and develop a growing sensitivity to the element of time in your workouts. If you can't see the pace clock because of visual difficulties, you may want to use a waterproof watch with a minute hand as a substitute timer. You can wear it, or you can put it around the lane line or under the starting block at the end of your swim lane, and use it as if it were a larger sweep pace clock.

POOL MARKINGS

SURFACE LANE LINES

Surface lane lines (Figure 4-5) are made of plastic floats on a wire cable and divide a swimming pool into lanes that are 6, 6½, 7, 7½, or 8 feet wide. When installed properly, they should fit snugly, anchored to bolts in the pool walls and tightened by means of adjustable end fittings. The colors of the floats are mixed in the center span of most surface lane lines, with solid colors for the last 15 feet at each end. The plastic floats are designed to break the turbulence caused by swimming and to keep the water surface as flat as possible.

Fitness swimmers need to establish traffic patterns within the lanes to maximize the use of the pool facility. One swimmer can swim alone right in the middle of the surface lane lines. Two swimmers can use the same lane if each keeps to his/her own side of the lane. Three or more swimmers can use the same lane if they "circle," going down one side of the lane and back along the other side. These swimmers would have to space themselves within the lane (at least 5–8 yards apart) to reduce the chance of swimming up on each other. Occasionally, they might have to delay a push-off, or let a faster swimmer pass on a turn, to keep the traffic pattern going smoothly within the lane. The system of circling works best when swimmers of similar speed or ability are grouped together within the same lane. Swimmers should never sit or hang on the surface lane lines, since the end fittings can be ruined or the cable snapped due to the extra tension and weight.

BACKSTROKE FLAGS

Backstroke flags (Figure 4-5) are suspended across the pool approximately 7 feet over the surface and exactly 15 feet from the wall. There must be at least three triangular pennants of two or more alternating colors over each lane. Each pennant should be 6–12 inches wide and 12–18 inches long. The flags enable backstroke swimmers to anticipate their turn or finish. Good swimmers will pass under the flags and then be able to count the number of strokes necessary to bring themselves to a hand touch against the wall. Less-skilled swimmers will pass under the flags and then look over one shoulder for the wall once or twice prior to the hand touch.

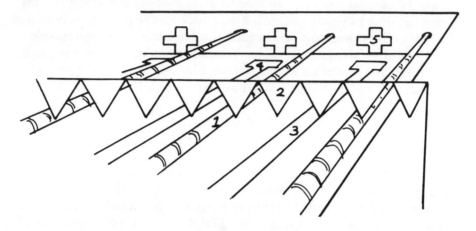

Figure 4-5. Pool markings: (*1*) surface lane line, (*2*) backstroke flag, (*3*) bottom lane line, (*4*) end of lane line, (*5*) target.

BOTTOM LANE LINES

Bottom lane lines (Figure 4-5) run along the pool bottom in the exact middle between the surface lane lines. They are highly visible because they are a distinct contrasting color to the rest of the pool bottom. Competitive standards require that the bottom lane lines be 12 inches wide and end in a T shape 5 feet from the wall. The T at each end of the bottom lane line is centered, and is 3 feet by 12 inches in dimension.

Bottom lane lines enable fitness swimmers to swim straight, to anticipate the turn or finish, and to maintain a traffic pattern within the lane. If alone in the lane, you can swim right over the bottom lane line. If there are two in the lane, stay on the same side of the bottom lane line on your way across the pool and on your way back. If there are three or more in the lane in a circling pattern, stay on the same side of the bottom lane line on your way across the pool and on the opposite side on your way back.

TARGETS

A cross-shaped target (Figure 4-5) is centered on the pool wall in each lane. The target is the same width and color as the bottom lane line, a distinct contrasting color to the rest of the pool wall. The horizontal segment of the target is 36 inches wide, and the vertical segment extends down at least 4 feet on the pool wall. The target is another visual indicator to help the swimmer anticipate the turn or finish.

38

REVIEW

Rate yourself as honestly and accurately as you can on the following checklist for equipment use:

SKILL	IMPROVE-MENT NEEDED	ADE-QUATE	GOOD
use of			
goggles	———	———	———
pull buoy	———	———	———
kickboard	———	———	———
hand paddles	———	———	———
swim fins	———	———	———
any other devices that you use regularly			
———	———	———	———
———	———	———	———
———	———	———	———
———	———	———	———
pace clock	———	———	———
following traffic patterns within the lane lines	———	———	———
use of pool markings to help with your turns	———	———	———

Continue to work in the pool on improving your weaknesses. Set some long-term goals for skill improvement and tailor your fitness swimming workouts to help you reach those goals. Use this checklist once or twice a year to chart your progress.

CHAPTER FIVE
Swimming Strokes

Fitness swimmers should use several different swimming strokes during their workouts as another means of adding variety to their training programs. Although the energy expeditures required to swim the different strokes are not the same, the potential fitness benefits of each stroke depend largely on the individual swimmer's intensity and pace.

Six swimming strokes are illustrated (in Figures 5-1 through 5-6) and described in this chapter in terms of the hand and arm movements, the foot and leg movements, the method of breathing, and the coordination of the entire stroke. Although this chapter should be helpful to fitness swimmers, it is not intended to be an exhaustive treatment of swimming technique. Many factors contribute to a "good stroke," and different swimmers will display slightly different but effective techniques in all strokes.

BUTTERFLY STROKE

PULLING ACTION

The hands enter the water at shoulder width or a little wider, with a very slight bend in the elbows.

The hands move down and back under the elbows ("high elbow position") just before strong movements of the shoulder joints pull both arms backward.

During this double arm pull, the upper arms and elbows point away from the sides of the body, and the distance between the hands varies with the amount of bend in the elbows at different points in the underwater stroke.

Just before the completion of the underwater pull, the hands may move slightly closer to each other before moving out to the side and forward over the surface of the water in the recovery.

The hands recover just over and somewhat parallel to the surface of the water, with the palms down or facing the surface. Although the recovery is wide, the elbows are slightly bent as the hands return to the entry position.

KICKING ACTION

Both feet and legs move up and down at the same time, and the knees bend and extend as the primary emphasis is on kicking down and back in a vertical plane with the feet and toes pointed.

The heels may cause some splashing as they break the water surface at the completion/start of each kick. There is an undulating action to this "dolphin" kick, and the hips will move up and down in reaction to the movements of the feet and legs.

BREATHING PATTERN

As the hands and arms move backward underwater and become even with the shoulders, lift your head to breathe. The face looks forward during the breathing, and the head is lifted only high enough to get a breath.

In general, you should breathe every second stroke in order to distort the body position the least and to fit the rhythm of this stroke the best. This pattern completes the breathing in time for the recovery of the hands and arms. As the hands go forward, the head should go back down into the water.

STROKE COORDINATION

The hand action should be continuous without any stopping of the hands at their entry into or exit from the water. Hand speed varies, however, and the hands accelerate as they move backward against the water.

Usually, there are two dolphin kicks per arm cycle: one as the hands enter the water and one at the completion of the underwater pull. Some good swimmers use just one kick, and many show a major kick followed by a minor or trail kick. Any of these patterns are acceptable.

The hands move at the same time and the feet move at the same time. Set the rhythm of the stroke primarily with the hands and arms, and then let the kick fit into that stroke rhythm.

When properly done, the breathing pattern and the hand action should blend together very smoothly. As the hands pull back, the head lifts forward to breathe. As the hands recover forward, the head goes back down into the water.

Although the body position is flat from side to side, there are some up-and-down movements of the shoulders, trunk, and hips as the swimmer moves forward through the water in an undulating pattern.

SPECIAL NOTE

The difficulty of this stroke is greatly exaggerated—thinking about it is worse than actually doing it. There are great similarities between the stroking patterns for the crawl and the butterfly. For most swimmers, crawl stroke is their best-developed stroke. So, you can build your new butterfly upon the well-established movements of the crawl stroke.

Learn the butterfly stroke over short distances first, maybe just one-quarter, one-third, or one-half lengths at the beginning. Swim it for a short distance, and then switch to the dolphin kick or back to crawl stroke for a while, or just rest a

two dolphin kicks per arm cycle

Swimming Strokes

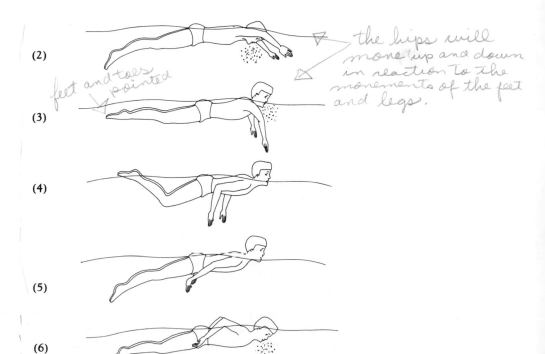

(1)

(2)

the hips will move up and down in reaction to the movements of the feet and legs.

(3)

feet and toes pointed

(4)

(5)

(6)

kick

(7)

(8)

Figure 5-1. Butterfly Stroke.

1. *Enter with hands at shoulder-width.*
2. *Start double arm pull.*
3. *Begin to lift head up for breathing.*
4. *Finish breathing. Bend knees prior to kick.*
5. *Finish kick and arm pull.*
6. *Arms recover to the side and forward.*
7. *Arms continue forward. Bend knees prior to kick.*
8. *Finish kick and return to shoulder-width entry.*

minute before trying the fly again. Swim it while you're fresh and can maintain the stroke rhythm, and rest frequently.

Build yourself up very gradually. Do just a little butterfly each time you swim, and you'll be amazed at how quickly and well this stroke can develop. Most importantly, *slow down when learning the butterfly stroke.* Don't discourage yourself with initial exhausting attempts. Move your hands slowly. Feel yourself move forward as your hands move back. Keep your kick going. Swim a short distance without even breathing to see what this stroke feels like. Gradually, add in an every-other-stroke breathing pattern. You can't learn this stroke by attacking it hard and fast.

Two of our Masters swimmers have developed their butterfly strokes in this gradual manner, and then gone on to swim the butterfly slowly over long distances. Both are good swimmers, but neither had extensive background in competitive swimming or in the butterfly stroke. The man has done 1,000 yards (40 lengths) of butterfly continuously, and the woman has done 2,500 yards (100 lengths) of butterfly continuously. You too can do this stroke!

BACKSTROKE

PULLING ACTION

The hand enters the water just slightly outside the width of the shoulders, with the arm straight and the hand turned out so the little-finger edge of the hand goes into the water first.

At the start of the underwater pull, the hand moves out to the side and even with the elbow (modification of the high elbow position). The hand and arm are pulled through by means of a strong shoulder-joint movement.

The elbow is bent during this propulsive action, and this single arm pull is done with the hand 4–8 inches beneath the water surface, with the hand moving somewhat parallel to the surface of the water.

As the pull is completed and the hand passes the hip, the elbow straightens and the hand and arm move upward (thumb-side first) into a vertical recovery. The elbow remains straight as the arm returns over the water to the entry position.

KICKING ACTION

The legs alternate in their kicking action as the feet move up and down. The toes should be pointed, and the knees should bend and extend with the primary emphasis on kicking backward and upward. The depth of the kick might be from 8 to 15 inches in a vertical plane.

The knees should not be lifted above the water surface, and you should concentrate on splashing the feet slightly to ensure a level body position. The feet should not be lifted above the surface of the water.

BREATHING PATTERN

Because the face is above the water surface during this stroke, you can breathe in through the mouth whenever you wish but on a regular cycle. Exhale through the nose (some from the mouth) whenever you're not inhaling.

A small amount of water is usually carried upward by the arm in the recovery. This water can splash in the swimmer's face and be very upsetting to a swimmer just beginning to learn this stroke. Using goggles and exhaling through your nose help, but if you continue to practice this stroke, in time you'll become less sensitive to this problem.

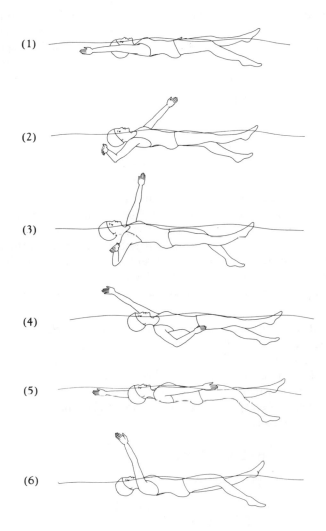

(1)

(2)

(3)

(4)

(5)

(6)

Figure 5-2. Backstroke

1. *Right arm enters the water. Maintain alternating kick.*
2. *Left arm recovers. Right arm pulls underwater.*
3. *Level body position. Shoulders turn (rotate or roll) in coordination with right arm pull and left arm recovery.*
4. *Pull and recovery almost finished.*
5. *Right arm recovers. Left arm enters the water.*
6. *Continue left arm pull (not visible) and right arm recovery to entry position.*

STROKE COORDINATION

Head and body position are very important in this stroke. Keep your chin up in a normal position, keep the back of your head in the water (not head back), keep your ears underwater, and keep your chest and stomach up. Don't sit in the water. Look straight up at the ceiling and kick up.

Maintain an alternating hand action. That is, when one arm is pulling, the other arm is recovering, and vice versa. The hand action should be continuous, although hand speed varies at different points in the arm cycle. The hand speed accelerates throughout the underwater pull and this momentum is then redirected into the over-the-surface recovery.

For most swimmers, the pull is more important than the kick. Keep your feet moving, but set the rhythm of the stroke primarily with the hands and arms. The kick contributes some to propulsion but helps mostly to maintain body position. Keep the kick going, but don't worry too much about the number of kicks per arm cycle—2-beat, 4-beat, and 6-beat kicks have all been successful for different swimmers.

While the swimmer remains horizontal from head to feet while moving through the water, there is considerable shoulder turning. That is, when the right hand is up high in the recovery, the right shoulder is visible just above the water surface; at the same time, when the left hand is pulling underwater, the left shoulder is down just beneath the water surface; and vice versa. In other words, don't swim flat from side to side—the shoulders should turn or roll in coordination with the pulling (on one side) and the recovery (on the other side) of the arms.

Some swimmers dislike the backstroke because they get disoriented while swimming on their back. They feel unsure of themselves because they are "upside-down-going-backward." To deal with this problem you might try moving periodically to a vertical position in the water as you try this stroke, taking short breaks to reorient yourself. Mostly, the problem is resolved by continuing to practice this stroke, giving yourself time to become accustomed to what was initially an awkward experience.

BREASTSTROKE

PULLING ACTION

In the starting position, the hands reach forward side by side, just beneath the water surface, with the arms fully extended.

The hands separate, moving out to the side and down to create the high elbow position in this stroke. The path of the hands is quite wide before the hands circle in under the face or neck.

The elbows move down under the shoulders and then continue forward, and the hands reach forward in the underwater recovery of the arms back to the starting position.

KICKING ACTION

The starting position for the kick is with the legs fully extended and near the surface of the water. The main objective is to push backward with the bottoms of the feet and with the inside edges of the feet and ankles.

The knees bend considerably, and the hips bend slightly, to recover the feet up near the buttocks. At this point, do not hold the knees tightly together, and do not let the knees get too wide apart and point out to the sides. The knees should be about a hand's width (or just slightly more than that) apart.

The feet are hooked (toes drawn up toward the shins) and then turned outward. The width of the feet at this point is greater than the width of the knees. All these previously described movements simply get the feet in position and ready to apply force backward.

When viewed from the top, the path of the feet in the propulsive part of this kick is slightly out, back, and then together in a long, flat curve. When viewed from the side, the path of the feet is primarily in a horizontal plane, although the feet may finish a little lower than their starting point in this propulsive action. Propulsion results from strong extension movements of the knees and hips.

The recovery of the legs (bending the knees, turning the feet out) should be done somewhat more slowly than the propulsive action (pushing backward with the feet).

BREATHING PATTERN

Begin to breathe to the front when the hands are wide in the high elbow position. The breathing can be completed as the elbows move down under the shoulders and then, without pausing, continue forward. Lift the head just high enough to get a breath.

This timing of the breathing pattern creates a natural link between the downward action of the arms and the lift to the front for the breath. It permits the arm action and the breathing to blend together so well that there is no hesitation or hitch in the arm stroke to complete the breathing. After the breath, the face goes back down into the water as the hands go forward to a fully stretched-out position.

It seems to fit the rhythm of this stroke best if the swimmer breathes once every stroke. There is some natural up-and-down movement as you swim this stroke, and this results from the synchrony between "elbows down," "head up," "hands forward," and "head down."

STROKE COORDINATION

The basic coordination of this stroke can be simply expressed: first you pull, then you kick, then you stretch out (brief glide or ride forward).

The relative contributions of the pull and the kick are more equal in this stroke than in the butterfly, crawl, and backstroke. For many swimmers, their power is split 50–50 between the pull and the kick.

(1)

(2)

(3)

(4)

(5)

(6)

(7)

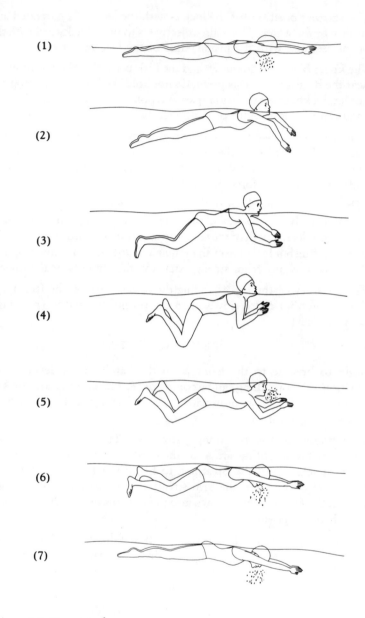

Figure 5-3. Breaststroke

1. *Glide position.*
2. *Arms circle out and back.*
3. *Arms sweep in. Breathing begins. Legs begin to bend.*
4. *Breathing completed. Arms circle in and forward. Legs still bending.*
5. *Legs kick back. Arms stretch forward. Head starts down.*
6. *Face down in the water. Full reach with arms. Kick is finishing.*
7. *Glide position.*

A maximum reach forward with the hands is very important because it gives the feet a chance to finish the kick and to contribute more to the total propulsion. This concept has often been described as a brief glide or ride forward. A more descriptive phrase might be "stretch-out," as the hands reach all the way forward, a position similar to hanging from a chinning bar while looking at your hands which are close together.

A primary objective in this stroke is to create as smooth a transition of power from your arms to your legs as possible. One of the challenges of this stroke is to reduce to a minimum the periods of sudden deceleration which follow the periods of acceleration, creating more even and efficient movement through the water.

Hand and foot speed are more variable in this stroke than in the other competitive strokes (fly, back, and crawl) due to the fact that the propulsive and recovery movements all occur underwater. The changing velocities and changing directions of the hands and feet in this stroke require the swimmer to have a good sense of timing.

CRAWL STROKE

PULLING ACTION

The hand enters the water fingertips first in front of the shoulder, with a slight bend in the elbow.

The hand moves down and back under the elbow (high elbow position) just before a strong movement of the shoulder joint pulls the arm backward.

During the single arm pull, the upper arm and elbow point away from the side of the body, and the amount of bend in the elbow varies at different points in the underwater stroke.

At the completion of the underwater pull, the hand moves upward and sideward into the recovery. The elbow bends during the recovery to create a high elbow position over the surface of the water as the hand returns to the entry position.

KICKING ACTION

The legs alternate in their kicking action as the feet move up and down. The toes should be pointed, and the knees should bend and extend with the primary emphasis on kicking backward and downward. The depth of the kick might be from 8 to 15 inches in a vertical plane.

The splashing action of the feet is caused by the heels breaking the surface of the water, and this promotes a level body position in the stroke. The feet should not be lifted up above the surface of the water.

BREATHING PATTERN

Chapter 3 contains great detail on the alternate side breathing patterns in crawl stroke, and readers are referred to that chapter for full descriptions, learning sequences, etc.

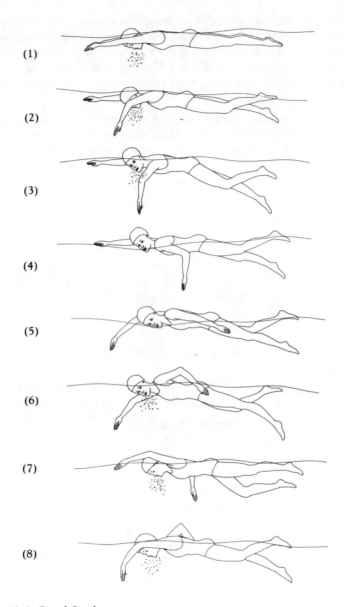

(1)

(2)

(3)

(4)

(5)

(6)

(7)

(8)

Figure 5-4. Crawl Stroke

1. *Full reach forward with arms.*
2. *Left arm pull begins. Maintain alternating kick.*
3. *Head begins to turn for breathing.*
4. *Breathing is begun.*
5. *Right arm pull begins as left arm pull finishes. Breathing is completed.*
6. *Shoulders turn (rotate or roll) in coordination with right arm pull, left arm recovery, and breathing.*
7. *Left arm enters the water and left arm pull begins as right arm pull finishes.*
8. *Right arm recovers as left arm pull continues.*

In brief, when the hand and arm move backward underwater and become even with the shoulder, turn to that side to breathe. This pattern completes the breathing in time for the recovery of the arm. When the arm moves over the surface of the water, the face turns back down into the water at the same time. When properly done, movements of the hands, arms, shoulders, neck, and head all blend together into one smooth action.

Fitness swimmers should experiment frequently with the many different breathing patterns that can be used in the crawl stroke.

STROKE COORDINATION

The hand action is alternating: when one arm pulls, the other arm recovers. The hand action should be continuous, with the hand speed accelerating throughout the underwater pull. This momentum is then redirected into the over-the-surface recovery.

For most swimmers, the pull is more important than the kick. Keep your feet moving, but set the rhythm of the stroke primarily with the hands and arms. The kick contributes some to propulsion but helps mostly to maintain body position. Keep the kick going, but don't worry too much about the number of kicks per arm cycle. Two-beat and 4-beat kicks have typically been associated with distance crawl stroke; 6-beat and 8-beat kicks are often used in sprint crawl stroke.

While the swimmer remains horizontal from head to feet as they move through the water, there is considerable shoulder turning. That is, when the right hand is up in the recovery, the right shoulder is visible just above the water surface; at the same time, when the left hand is pulling underwater, the left shoulder is down just beneath the water surface; and vice versa. In other words, don't swim flat from side to side—the shoulders should turn or roll in coordination with the pulling (on one side) and the recovery (on the other side) of the arms.

ELEMENTARY BACKSTROKE

PULLING ACTION

The hand and arm action in this stroke can be simply described as "up-out-together." From their starting/gliding position by the sides of the legs, the hands recover up the sides of the body and then outward slightly above shoulder level.

The propulsive action is a double arm pull, with the elbows slightly bent and with the hands moving parallel to the water surface at a depth of 4–6 inches.

As the pull is completed and the hands pass the hips, the elbows straighten in a definite push and the hands return to the starting/gliding position with the palms facing the sides of the legs.

KICKING ACTION

The starting/gliding position for the kick is with the legs fully extended and near the surface of the water. The main objective is to push backward with the bottoms of the feet and with the inside edges of the feet and ankles.

51

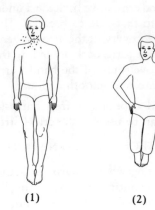

(1)   (2)

(3)
(4)

(5)   (6)

Figure 5-5. Elementary Backstroke

1.   *Glide position.*
2.   *Arms move up and knees bend.*
3.   *Arms move out and feet turn out.*
4.   *Arms and legs are ready to pull and kick.*
5.   *Double arm pull, and inverted breaststroke kick.*
6.   *Return to glide position.*

52

The knees bend about 90 degrees, dropping the feet beneath the knees. At this point, do not hold the knees tightly together, and do not let the knees get too wide apart and point out to the sides. The knees should be about a hand's width (or just slightly more than that) apart.

The feet are hooked (toes drawn up toward the shins) and then turned outward. The width of the feet at this point is greater than the width of the knees. All these previously described movements simply get the feet in position and ready to apply force backward.

When viewed from the top, the path of the feet in the propulsive part of this kick is slightly out, back, and then together in a long, flat curve. When viewed from the side, the path of the feet is primarily upward to the surface. Propulsion results from strong extension movements of the knee.

BREATHING PATTERN

For most swimmers, a natural pattern is to breathe in during the recovery phase and breathe out during the propulsive phase of this stroke.

STROKE COORDINATION

Head and body position are very important in this stroke. Keep your chin up in a normal position, keep the back of your head in the water (not head back), keep your ears underwater, and keep your chest and stomach up. Don't sit in the water. Look straight up at the ceiling.

The recoveries of the arms and legs occur at the same time, as do the propulsive movements of the arms and legs. The feet may finish the kick just before the hands finish the pull because the feet move through slightly less distance than the hands do. The hands, feet, and knees should remain underwater, and there should be no splashing in this stroke.

The recovery of the arms and legs (arms up, knees bent—arms out to the sides, feet turned out) should be done somewhat more slowly than the propulsive action (double arm pull, outward-backward-upward kick).

The speed of the hands and feet accelerate during the propulsive pull and kick, and this momentum is then dissipated into a short glide with the hands by your sides and the feet together. When the momentum of the glide slows down, the next recovery of the arms and legs begins. If you are using this stroke as a resting stroke, you can maintain the glide a little longer. If you are using this stroke as a fitness stroke, you can minimize the glide in order to swim faster.

SIDESTROKE

PULLING ACTION

The starting/gliding position is on your side with the bottom arm stretched out reaching forward in the water and the top arm near the body stretched out toward the feet.

The propulsive action of the bottom arm and hand is parallel to the surface of the water. The elbow is bent and the hand moves in front of the body and down

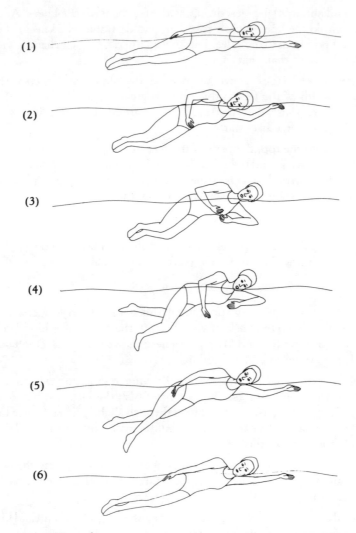

Figure 5-6. Sidestroke

1. *Glide position.*
2. *Left arm pull begins as right arm recovers. Knees bend.*
3. *Hands pass each other as knees bend more.*
4. *Wide scissors kick. Right arm pushes backward as left arm recovers forward.*
5. *The right arm push, the left arm reach, and the kick all finish at the same time.*
6. *Return to glide position.*

to the level of the lower chest. At the same time, the top arm recovers to the level of the middle chest by bending the elbow.

The hands pass each other and then return to their starting/gliding positions. The bottom arm recovers forward close to the chest and shoulder. At the same time, the top arm pushes down past the hip by straightening the elbow in its propulsive action.

KICKING ACTION

Because of the resemblance, this kick is called the scissors kick. The starting/gliding position for this kick is on the side with the legs fully extended and near the surface of the water.

The legs recover by bending the knees and hips, and then the feet separate wide apart. Propulsion results from squeezing the legs together, back to the starting/gliding position. The leg and foot action throughout the kick is horizontal and parallel.

Ideally, the top leg should go forward (towards the front) during this kick. However, the kick and stroke can also be done successfully with the top leg moving backward (inverted scissors kick).

BREATHING PATTERN

For most swimmers, a natural pattern is to breathe in as the hands approach each other and the legs recover, and to breathe out as the hands stretch out into the glide and the scissors kick occurs.

STROKE COORDINATION

Head and body position are very important in this stroke. You must stay on your side. Turning on the back or stomach distorts this stroke greatly. Mostly, you should look sideward and backward while swimming this stroke. Occasionally, you may glance forward to check your direction or distance to the wall.

The basic sequence for the coordination of this stroke is as follows: the bottom arm is propulsive as the top arm and both legs recover; the bottom arm recovers as the top arm and both legs are propulsive; then stretch out in the starting/gliding position. The hands and feet remain in the water, and there should be no splashing in this stroke. The recovery of the arms and legs should be done somewhat more slowly than the propulsive actions.

You should learn to swim this stroke on either side. This requires some work on the kick, as the direction of the legs will naturally change when you turn over onto the other side. Count the number of strokes for one length on each side, and work to make them as equal as possible.

The speed of the hands and feet accelerate during the propulsive actions, and this momentum is then dissipated into a short glide. When the momentum of the glide slows down, the next stroke begins. If you are using this stroke as a resting stroke, you can maintain the glide a little longer. If you are using this stroke as a fitness stroke, you can minimize the glide in order to swim faster.

REVIEW

Rate yourself as honestly and accurately as you can on the following checklist of in-the-water skills:

SKILL	IMPROVE- MENT NEEDED	ADE- QUATE	GOOD
butterfly stroke			
pull	_____	_____	_____
kick	_____	_____	_____
breathing	_____	_____	_____
coordination	_____	_____	_____
backstroke			
pull	_____	_____	_____
kick	_____	_____	_____
breathing	_____	_____	_____
coordination	_____	_____	_____
breaststroke			
pull	_____	_____	_____
kick	_____	_____	_____
breathing	_____	_____	_____
coordination	_____	_____	_____
crawl stroke			
pull	_____	_____	_____
kick	_____	_____	_____
breathing	_____	_____	_____
coordination	_____	_____	_____
elementary backstroke			
pull	_____	_____	_____
kick	_____	_____	_____
breathing	_____	_____	_____
coordination	_____	_____	_____
sidestroke			
pull	_____	_____	_____
kick	_____	_____	_____
breathing	_____	_____	_____
coordination	_____	_____	_____
both sides	_____	_____	_____

Continue to work in the pool on improving your weaknesses. Set some long-term goals for skill improvement and tailor your fitness swimming workouts to help you reach those goals. Use this checklist once or twice a year to chart your progress.

CHAPTER SIX
Push-offs and Turns

Fitness swimmers must learn the proper techniques for push-offs and turns in order to use a swimming pool correctly and efficiently. These skills may be practiced in special sessions at the start or finish of your workout, as a break in the middle of a longer workout, and throughout the entire workout as you turn around to begin the next length. Good push-offs and turns cut down the actual distance swum during each length, and thereby improve your speed. More importantly, they give momentum to the stroke being swum that can be carried throughout the rest of the length.

PUSH-OFFS

The basic component of all the turns is the underwater push-off on the front or on the back. The goal is simply to be able to push and glide underwater in a streamlined body position for 2–3 body lengths.

Instructions for the *front push-off* (Figure 6-1) are as follows:

The starting position on the pool wall is one hand grasping the wall, both feet on the wall, shoulders underwater, one hand stretched out in front, and looking forward over the outstretched hand.

From that position, let go of the wall and go underwater 6–10 inches.

While underwater on the front, bring your hands together overhead with the elbows straight and the arms covering the ears.

Push forcefully with your feet and legs to perform the push and glide underwater. Don't pull or kick. Simply glide in a streamlined position, stretched out from your fingertips to your toes. Follow a very slight angle upward to the surface.

Be sure that you are exhaling through your nose during the entire time that you are underwater. This is evidence of breath control and will prevent water from entering the nose.

If you are wearing swim goggles, look straight forward at the start of the push-off. After the initial momentum of the push-off has passed, readjust the head position down so that the ears are covered by the straight arms, and continue to glide.

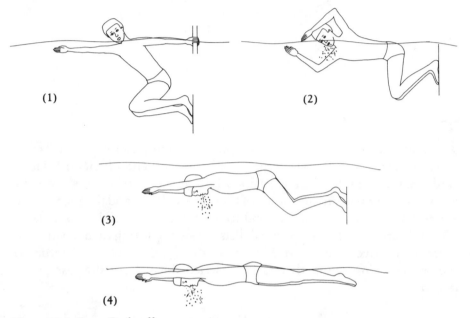

Figure 6-1. Front Push-off

1. *Starting position. Breathe in.*
2. *Let go of wall, bringing one arm over, and go underwater. Exhale.*
3. *Bring hands together and push forcefully with legs and feet.*
4. *Glide position.*

Instructions for the *back push-off* (Figure 6-2) are as follows:

The starting position, facing the pool wall, is both hands grasping the wall, both feet on the wall, and shoulders underwater.

From that position, let go of the wall and go underwater 6–10 inches.

While underwater on the back, move your arms sideward and bring your hands together overhead with the elbows straight and the arms covering the ears.

Push forcefully with your feet and legs to perform the push and glide underwater. Don't pull or kick. Simply glide in a streamlined position, stretched out from your fingertips to your toes. Follow a very slight angle upward to the surface.

Be sure that you are exhaling through your nose during the entire time that you are underwater. This is evidence of breath control and will prevent water from entering the nose.

If you are wearing swim goggles, keep the chin down slightly at the start of the push-off. After the initial momentum of the push-off has passed, readjust the head position (look up) so that the ears are covered by the straight arms, and continue to glide.

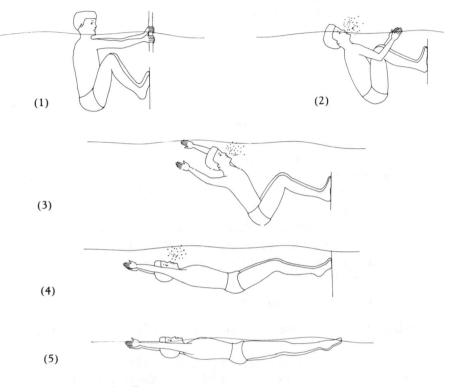

Figure 6-2. Back Push-off

1. *Starting position. Breathe in.*
2. *Release hands and go underwater. Exhale.*
3. *Arms move underwater to the sides over your head.*
4. *Bring hands together and push forcefully with legs and feet.*
5. *Glide position.*

Whether on the front or on the back, the sequence should be (1) starting position, (2) go underwater, (3) hands together, (4) push, and (5) glide. Beginners tend to make the mistake of pushing off before the hands are together and stretched overhead, or the related mistake of pushing off with the hands together but then quickly pulling them through to the sides during the glide. Don't push off until the hands are together overhead, and don't ruin the glide by destroying this straight and stretched position. Ultimately, stroking movements of the hands and arms will begin from this streamlined position—so keep the hands together and arms stretched out overhead during the glide.

Beginners may also go too deep if they lift the shoulders up just before releasing the hand grip(s) on the wall and then plunge straight down underwater before pushing off, or if they push off at a slightly downward angle toward the bottom. To avoid this mistake, keep your shoulders underwater or near the surface as you start the push-off. Your feet should be 18–24 inches beneath the water surface (not near the gutter) as you push against the pool wall.

STROKE TURNS

In the stroke turns, the swimmer approaches the wall swimming one type of stroke, turns, and leaves the wall swimming the same stroke. In addition to using these turns throughout your entire workout, you may practice them in the pool by starting about 5 yards out from the wall, swimming in to the wall and turning, pushing off underwater, and then taking one or two surface strokes. In this special practice, the emphasis is on the turn and push-off, not on swimming very long distances with the different strokes.

The various stroke turns are described in the following sections. Note that for those turns requiring a one-hand touch at the wall, swimmers should practice using either hand, so that they can turn off the right hand or left hand equally well.

BUTTERFLY TURN

The butterfly turn (Figure 6-3) is also known as fly-to-fly, or fly in–fly out.

Swim in toward the wall with the butterfly stroke and touch the wall with both hands (not necessarily on the same level, but at the same time).

Tuck the knees up toward your chest and swing the feet to the wall as you turn away from the wall, planting the feet firmly against the side of the pool. Don't climb up the wall just before or as you turn around—keep the shoulders near the surface of the water.

You can breathe naturally as you turn around. Many swimmers keep one arm under the surface as they turn, and bring the other arm over the surface. This contributes to the turning action, and the swimmer breathes in deeply to the side as the top arm comes over.

Perform an underwater push and glide on the front. As the speed of the glide diminishes, take one or two dolphin kicks before pulling the hands through for the first arm stroke as you approach the surface.

Good swimmers will usually keep their head down for the first arm stroke, and then breathe on the second stroke as they continue swimming away from the wall on the surface with the butterfly stroke.

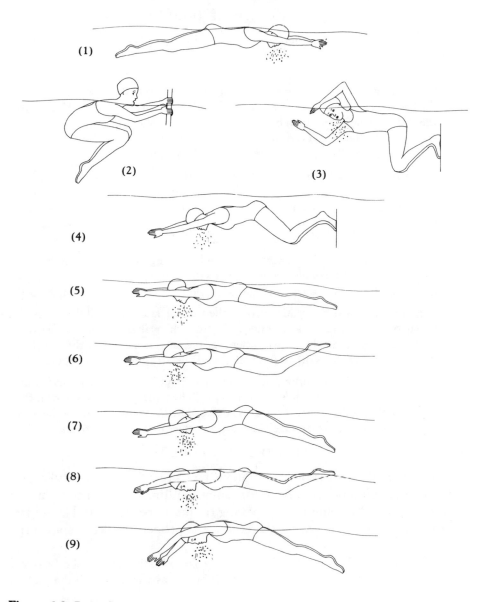

Figure 6-3. Butterfly Turn

1. *Swim in to a two-hand touch.*
2. *Tuck up. Feet swing in to the wall. Lift head to breathe.*
3. *Bring one arm over and go underwater. Exhale.*
4. *Bring hands together. Strong leg push.*
5. *Glide position.*
6. *Begin kick.*
7. *Take first dolphin kick.*
8. *Begin second dolphin kick.*
9. *Start double arm pull.*

BACKSTROKE TURN

The backstroke turn (Figure 6-4) is also known as back-to-back, or back in–back out.

Swim in toward the wall with the backstroke. Good swimmers will swim under the backstroke flags (which are suspended 15 feet from the wall and 7 feet over the water surface) and then be able to count the strokes in to their hand touch on the wall. Inexperienced swimmers will glance over one shoulder as they approach the wall in preparation for their hand touch.

The hand touch is with one hand only, with the hand turned down. As the hand grasps the wall, turn toward that hand onto your stomach and then grasp the wall with the other hand also. With both hands holding the wall, tuck the knees up toward your chest and swing the feet in to the wall. Keep the shoulders near the surface and plant both feet firmly against the side of the pool.

Breathe in deeply, and then perform an underwater push and glide on the back. Be sure to exhale through the nose during the entire push-off. As the speed of the glide diminishes, start to flutter kick while underwater on your back.

Pull one arm through as you approach the surface, and then pull the other arm through as you continue swimming away from the wall on the surface with the backstroke. You may breathe in whenever the face comes above the surface of the water as the push-off is completed and the stroking action begins.

Note: Some beginning fitness swimmers may elect to do the back push-off on the surface with their hands by their legs. When the glide slows down, they begin to kick and then start the arm stroke. The face remains above the water surface throughout the entire push-off and start of the back stroke.

ALTERNATE BACKSTROKE TURN

Although the backstroke turn shown in Figure 6-5 is commonly called a flip turn, it does not involve a true somersaulting action. The swimmer actually turns by spinning or pivoting on the upper back and shoulders rather than "flipping over"; therefore, it is properly called a spin turn.

Swim in toward the wall with the backstroke. Use the backstroke flags and count your strokes, or glance over one shoulder as you approach the wall, in preparation for your hand touch.

For this turn, the hand touch is with one hand only, as follows: the hand touches the side of the wall (no grasping) behind the head and shoulder, with the fingers pointed down, the palm against the wall, and with the elbow bent. Breathe in deeply as you touch the wall with your hand.

Without stopping and losing your momentum in toward the wall, tuck up and swing the knees and feet up and over the surface toward the hand that touched the wall. Stay on your back, and spin or pivot on your upper back and shoulders to turn around. If you touch with the right hand, spin or pivot to the right; if you touch with the left hand, spin or pivot to the left.

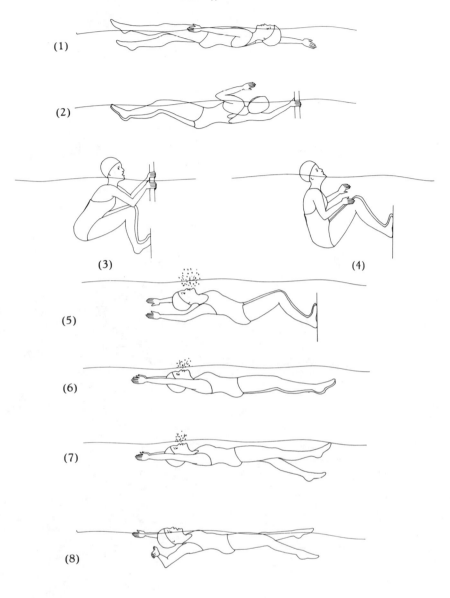

Figure 6-4. Backstroke Turn

1.   *Swim in to a one-hand touch.*
2.   *Turn over toward that hand.*
3.   *Tuck up. Feet swing in to the wall. Breathe in.*
4.   *Arms move underwater to the side over your head.*
5.   *Bring hands together. Strong leg push.*
6.   *Glide position.*
7.   *Start kick.*
8.   *Start single arm pull.*

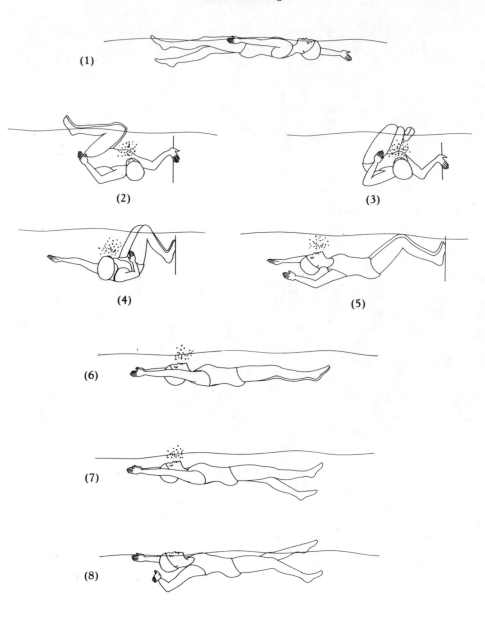

Figure 6-5. Alternate Backstroke Turn (Spin Turn)

1. *Swim in to a one-hand touch.*
2. *Tuck up. Knees and feet move up and over toward hand on wall.*
3. *Spin or pivot on your upper back and shoulders.*
4. *Feet to the wall.*
5. *Bring hands together. Strong leg push.*
6. *Glide position.*
7. *Start kick.*
8. *Start single arm pull.*

Usually, the face submerges during this spinning action, so continue to exhale through your nose during the entire underwater portion of this turn. As your knees and feet swing over the surface, the hand that was touching the wall may push a little against the wall to contribute to the pivoting action. Don't push too hard with the touching hand, especially if you're swimming slowly, or you'll push yourself too far away from the wall.

Once both feet are planted firmly against the side of the pool, perform an underwater push and glide on the back. Start to flutter kick, pull one arm and then the other as you continue swimming away from the wall on the surface with the backstroke. Breathe in after your face surfaces.

BREASTSTROKE TURN

The breaststroke turn shown in Figure 6-6 is also known as breast-to-breast, or breast in–breast out.

Swim in toward the wall with the breaststroke and touch the wall with both hands (not necessarily on the same level, but at the same time).

Tuck the knees up toward your chest and swing the feet to the wall as you turn away from the wall, planting both feet firmly against the side of the pool. Don't climb up the wall just before or as you turn around—keep the shoulders near the surface of the water.

You can breathe very naturally as you turn around. Many swimmers keep one arm under the surface as they turn, and bring the other arm over the surface. This contributes to the turning action, and the swimmer breathes in deeply to the side as the top arm comes over.

Perform an underwater push and glide on the front. As the speed of the glide diminishes, perform the following sequence: start the arm pull, lift the head to breathe, finish the kick, and stretch forward with your hands. Continue swimming away from the wall on the surface with the breaststroke.

ALTERNATE BREASTSTROKE TURN

The alternate breaststroke turn (Figure 6-7) involves an underwater pull-out, or double arm pull-through-and-push. This turn is performed in the same way as the regular breastroke turn until the push-off.

Perform an underwater push and glide on the front (a little deeper than for the other strokes). As the speed of the glide diminishes, pull both arms from over the head down past the hips (the pull-out, or double arm pull-through-and-push). Then glide again with your hands by your legs. As this second glide slows down, recover your hands forward and breaststroke kick up to the surface.

Some part of the head must be above the surface of the water before the next stroke can be started and the first breath can be taken. Continue swimming away from the wall on the surface with the breaststroke.

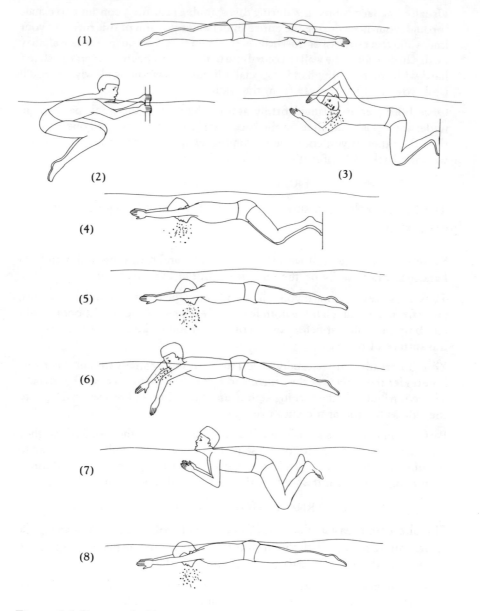

Figure 6-6. Breaststroke Turn

1. *Swim in to a two-hand touch.*
2. *Tuck up. Feet swing in to the wall. Lift head to breathe.*
3. *Bring one arm over and go underwater.*
4. *Bring hands together. Strong leg push.*
5. *Glide position.*
6. *Back of head above the surface. Start arm stroke.*
7. *Finish pull. Lift head to breathe. Start kick.*
8. *Finish kick. Face in the water. Reach forward.*

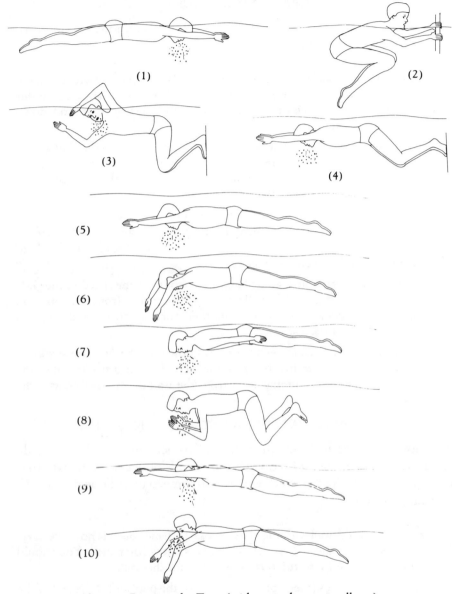

Figure 6-7. Alternate Breaststroke Turn (with an underwater pull-out)

1. *Swim in to a two-hand touch.*
2. *Tuck up. Feet swing in to the wall. Lift head to breathe.*
3. *Bring one arm over and go underwater.*
4. *Bring hands together. Strong leg push.*
5. *Glide position.*
6. *Start double arm pull-through underwater.*
7. *Finish double arm pull-through underwater. Short glide.*
8. *Hands forward. Kick up to the surface.*
9. *Reach forward. Back of head above the surface.*
10. *Start regular arm stroke.*

CRAWL STROKE TURN

The crawl stroke turn shown in Figure 6-8 is also known as crawl-to-crawl, or crawl in–crawl out.

Swim in toward the wall with the crawl stroke and touch the wall with one hand only. If you touch with the right hand, turn away from that hand, doing this turn to the left. If you touch with the left hand, turn away from that hand, doing this turn to the right.

Tuck the knees up toward your chest and swing the feet in to the wall as you turn away from the wall, planting both feet firmly against the side of the pool. Don't grasp the wall with the other hand and don't climb up the wall just before or as you turn around—keep the shoulders near the surface of the water.

You can breathe very naturally as you turn around. Many swimmers keep one arm under the surface as they turn, and bring the other arm over the surface. This contributes to the turning action, and the swimmer breathes in deeply to the side as the top arm comes over.

Perform an underwater push and glide on the front. As the speed of the glide diminishes, start to flutter kick while underwater on your front. Pull one arm through as you approach the surface, and then pull the other arm through to continue with the surface stroke.

Good swimmers will usually keep their head down for the first arm stroke or first arm cycle, waiting to breathe until the second or third stroke out of the turn as they continue swimming away from the wall on the surface with the crawl stroke.

ALTERNATE CRAWL STROKE TURN

The crawl stroke turn shown in Figure 6-9 is accurately and commonly called a flip turn because it involves a somersaulting action. The swimmer actually turns by "flipping over" with a half-somersault followed by a half-twisting push-off.

Swim in toward the wall with the crawl stroke. A hand touch is not necessary; only the feet touch the wall as the half-somersault is completed. You should take your last breath into the turn 3–5 feet from the wall.

Use the pool markings (the T on the bottom of the pool and at the end of the lane line, and the target on the side of the pool) to help you judge your distance from the wall. Pull one arm or both arms through to your sides after your last breath as you continue to move in toward the wall.

The distance from the wall (1–3 feet) at which you start the turn varies with your speed. If you flip your turn (somersault over) and your feet don't reach the wall, next time move in a little closer and/or swim a little faster into your turn.

Bend forward hard and fast to start the half-somersault. Although beginners tend to do this turn in a tight tuck position, more experienced swimmers

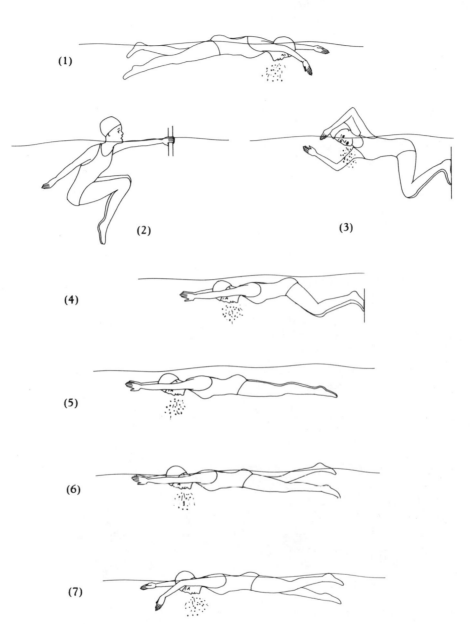

Figure 6-8. Crawl Stroke Turn

1.   Swim in to a one-hand touch.
2.   Tuck up. Feet swing in to the wall. Lift head to breathe.
3.   Bring one arm over and go underwater.
4.   Bring hands together. Strong leg push.
5.   Glide position.
6.   Start kick.
7.   Start single arm pull.

71

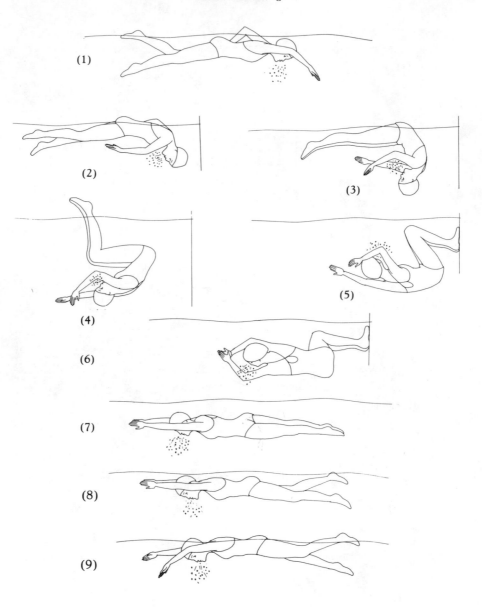

Figure 6-9. Alternate Crawl Stroke Turn (Flip Turn)

1. *Swim in. No hand touch.*
2. *Pull through. Quick kick. Begin somersault.*
3. *Continue somersault.*
4. *Finish somersault by tucking up more.*
5. *Plant feet firmly against the wall.*
6. *Bring hands together. Half-twist. Strong leg push.*
7. *Glide position.*
8. *Start kick.*
9. *Start single arm pull.*

perform this flip turn correctly in a semitucked position, bent over completely at the waist and hips with the knees partly bent. Many swimmers instinctively flutter kick or dolphin kick just before they turn over to assist with the somersaulting action.

You should somersault so that your feet land right against the wall. You are now underwater, on your back, looking up. Remember the importance of breath control during the underwater portion of the turn, and continue to exhale through the nose during the somersaulting, twisting, and pushing-off movements.

Perform a half-twisting underwater push and glide to get back onto your front. Start to flutter kick, and pull one arm and then the other as you continue swimming away from the wall with the crawl stroke. Wait until the second or third stroke to take your first breath out of the turn.

Beginners sometimes twist too soon in the turn, twisting in the middle of the somersault. This is usually caused by disorientation and by getting water up the nose. The two descriptive parts of the turn, a half-somersault and a half-twisting push-off, must be done separately in sequence.

If you have this problem, practice swimming in to the wall with the crawl stroke, flipping over, and then leaving the wall with the backstroke. As you become confident with the half-somersaulting action, gradually begin to add in the half-twisting push-off to get back on to the front with the crawl stroke.

NOTE: Remember that a well-executed crawl stroke turn is better than a poorly-done crawl stroke flip turn.

ELEMENTARY BACKSTROKE TURN

The elementary backstroke turn (Figure 6-10) is also known as elementary back-to-elementary back, or elementary back in–elementary back out.

Swim in toward the wall with the elementary backstroke. Use the backstroke flags and count your strokes, or glance over one shoulder as you approach the wall, in preparation for your hand touch.

The hand touch is with one hand only, with the hand turned down. As the hand grasps the wall, turn toward that hand onto your stomach and then grasp the wall with the other hand also. With both hands holding the wall, tuck the knees up toward your chest and swing the feet in to the wall. Keep the shoulders near the surface and plant both feet firmly against the side of the pool.

Breathe in deeply, and then perform an underwater push and glide on the back. Be sure to exhale through the nose during the entire push-off. As the speed of the glide diminishes, perform a long hand action which is a double arm pull-through-and-push, and then glide again with your hands by your legs. As this second glide slows down, recover your arms and legs and then continue swimming away from the wall on the surface with the elementary backstroke. Breathe in after your face surfaces.

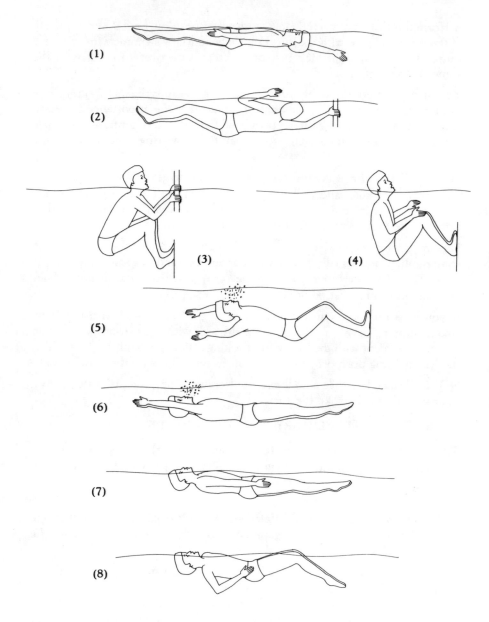

Figure 6-10. Elementary Backstroke Turn

1.   *Swim in to a one-hand touch.*
2.   *Turn over toward that hand.*
3.   *Tuck up. Feet swing in to the wall. Breathe in.*
4.   *Arms move underwater to the side over your head.*
5.   *Bring hands together. Strong leg push.*
6.   *Glide position.*
7.   *Finish double arm pull-through. Short glide.*
8.   *Start regular stroke.*

74

NOTE: Some beginning fitness swimmers may elect to do the back push-off on the surface with their hands by their legs. When the glide slows down, the swimmer recovers the arms and legs in preparation for the first pull and kick. The face remains above the water surface throughout the entire back push-off and start of the elementary backstroke.

SIDESTROKE TURN

The sidestroke turn (Figure 6-11) is also known as side-to-side, or side in–side out.

Swim in toward the wall with the sidestroke and touch the wall with your bottom hand. If you're swimming on your right side, grasp the wall with your right hand; if you're on your left side, touch with your left hand.

Tuck the knees up toward your chest and swing the feet to the wall as you turn away from the wall, planting both feet firmly against the side of the pool. Don't climb up the wall just before or as you turn around—keep the shoulders near the surface of the water.

You can breathe very naturally as you turn around. Many swimmers keep one arm under the surface as they turn, and bring the other arm over the surface. This contributes to the turning action, and the swimmer breathes in deeply to the side as the top arm comes over.

Perform an underwater push and glide on the front. As the speed of the glide diminishes, pull one arm through to your side as you turn onto the opposite side and continue to swim away from the wall on the surface with the sidestroke. For example, if you wish to swim away from the wall on your right side, pull your left arm through to your left side as you turn on to your right side, and then continue swimming the sidestroke on the right. To swim away on your left side, pull your right arm through and turn on to your left side, and then continue swimming on the left side.

INDIVIDUAL MEDLEY TURNS

In the individual medley turns, the swimmer approaches the wall swimming one type of stroke, turns, and leaves the wall swimming a different stroke. The 100-yard individual medley event (100 IM) consists of the butterfly, back, breast, and crawl strokes in that order, using each stroke for one-fourth of the total distance and using the IM turns exclusively. The longer individual medley events (200 IM and 400 IM) use both stroke and IM turns to complete the respective distances, with each stroke used for one-fourth of the total distance in the proper order.

In addition to using some IM swimming and the IM turns during your workout, you may do some special practice on these turns by starting about 5 yards from the wall, turning, and then taking a few surface strokes. Turns in other medley variations can be done by approaching the wall with one stroke, touching the wall and turning, and then leaving the wall with

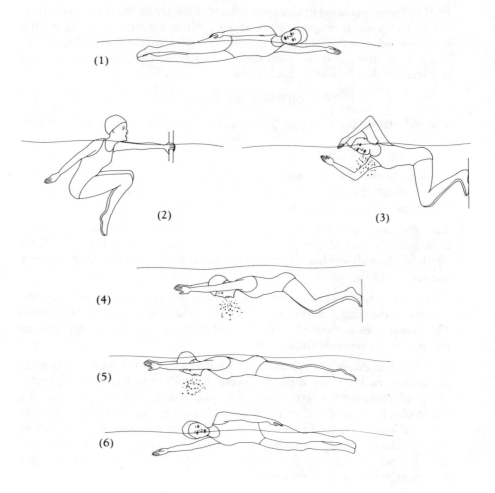

Figure 6-11. Sidestroke Turn

1. *Swim in to a one-hand touch.*
2. *Tuck up. Feet swing in to the wall. Breathe in.*
3. *Bring one arm over and go underwater.*
4. *Bring hands together. Strong leg push.*
5. *Glide position.*
6. *Pull one arm through, and turn onto the opposite side.*

the appropriate push-off for the new stroke, whatever it might be. The descriptions that follow have been abbreviated because they simply build on the previously described stroke turns.

BUTTERFLY-TO-BACK TURN

The butterfly-to-back turn (Figure 6-12) is also known as fly in–back out.

Swim in with the fly—touch with both hands—tuck up and swing the feet straight forward in to the wall—breathe in deeply—perform an underwater push and glide on the back—start to flutter kick—pull one arm, then the other—breathe in and swim away with the backstroke.

BACK-TO-BREAST TURN

The back-to-breast turn shown in Figure 6-13 is also known as back in – breast out.

Swim in with the backstroke—touch the wall with one hand only, with the hand turned down—turn to that side, tuck up and swing the feet in to the wall—breathe in deeply—perform an underwater push and glide on the front—pull, breathe, kick, stretch—swim away with the breaststroke.

ALTERNATE BACK-TO-BREAST TURN

The alternate back-to-breast turn (Figure 6-14) is also called the flip turn.

Swim in with the backstroke—touch the wall with one hand only, with the fingers pointed down, the palm to the wall, the elbow bent, and the hand behind the head and shoulder—breathe in deeply—tuck up and perform a straight, backward half-somersault so both feet wind up right against the wall— keep your eyes open during this half-somersault, and look for the lane line on the bottom of the pool to help reorient yourself after flipping over—continue to exhale through your nose during the entire underwater portion of this turn—perform an underwater push and glide on the front—pull, breathe, kick, stretch—swim away with the breaststroke.

NOTE: Both back-to-breast turns can also be performed with an underwater pull-out for the breaststroke as described on pp. 67 and 69.

BREAST-TO-CRAWL TURN

The breast-to-crawl turn (Figure 6-15) is also known as breast in–crawl out.)

Swim in with the breaststroke—touch with both hands—tuck up and swing the feet in to the wall as you turn away from the wall—breathe in deeply as one arm stays in the water and the other arm comes over the surface—perform an underwater push and glide on the front—start to flutter kick—pull one arm, then the other—breathe in on the second or third stroke as you swim away with the crawl stroke.

77

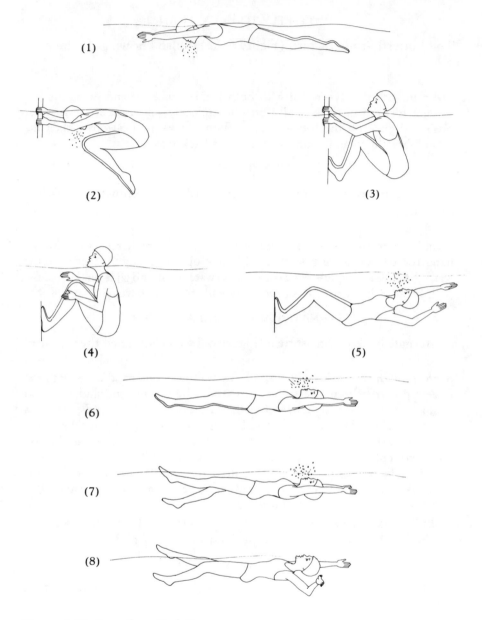

Figure 6-12. Butterfly-to-Back Turn

1. *Swim in to a two-hand touch.*
2. *Tuck up.*
3. *Feet swing in to the wall. Breathe in.*
4. *Arms move underwater to the side over your head.*
5. *Bring hands together. Strong leg push.*
6. *Glide position.*
7. *Start kick.*
8. *Start single arm pull.*

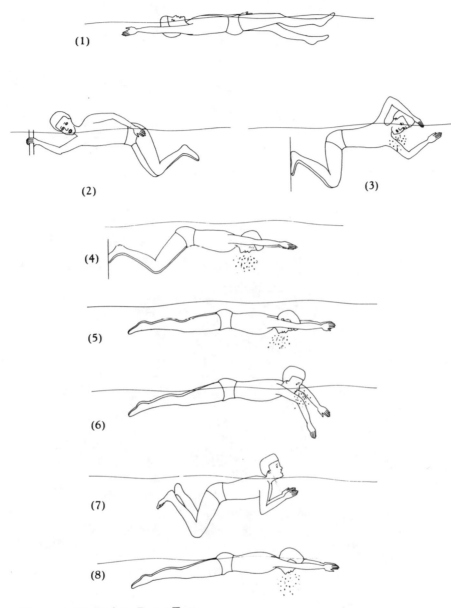

Figure 6-13. Back-to-Breast Turn

1. Swim in to a one-hand touch.
2. Turn to the side toward that hand. Tuck up. Feet swing in to the wall. Breathe in.
3. Bring one arm over and go underwater.
4. Bring hands together. Strong leg push.
5. Glide position.
6. Back of head above the surface. Start arm stroke.
7. Finish pull. Lift head to breathe. Start kick.
8. Finish kick. Face in the water. Reach forward.

79

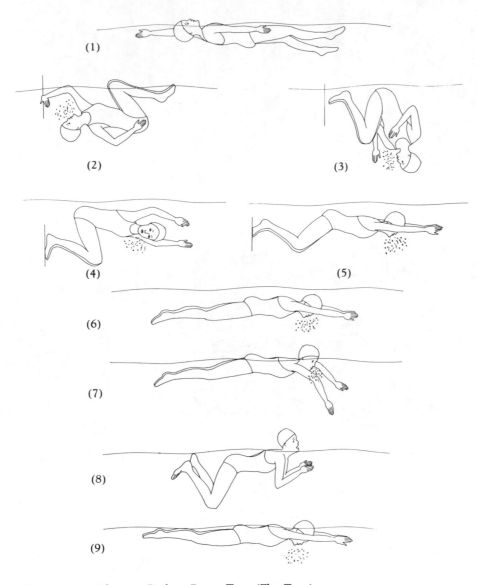

Figure 6-14. Alternate Back-to-Breast Turn (Flip Turn)

1. *Swim in to a one-hand touch.*
2. *Tuck up to start a back somersault.*
3. *Continue straight back tuck somersault. Look for lane line on pool bottom. Plant your feet firmly against the wall.*
4. *Bring hands together.*
5. *Strong leg push.*
6. *Glide position.*
7. *Back of head above the surface. Start arm stroke.*
8. *Finish pull. Lift head to breathe. Start kick.*
9. *Finish kick. Face in the water. Reach forward.*

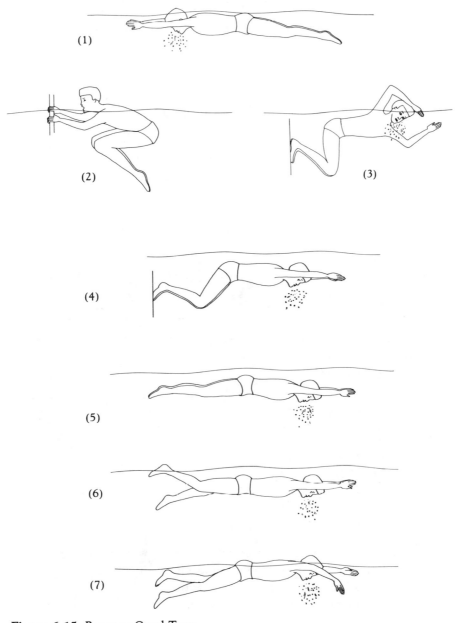

Figure 6-15. Breast-to-Crawl Turn

1. *Swim in to a two-hand touch.*
2. *Tuck up. Feet swing in to the wall. Lift head to breathe.*
3. *Bring one arm over and go underwater.*
4. *Bring hands together. Strong leg push.*
5. *Glide position.*
6. *Start kick.*
7. *Start single arm pull.*

81

REVIEW

Rate yourself as honestly and accurately as you can on the following checklist of the in-the-water skills:

SKILL	IMPROVE- MENT NEEDED	ADE- QUATE	GOOD
push-offs	———	———	———
on the front	———	———	———
on the back	———	———	———
stroke turns	———	———	———
butterfly turn	———	———	———
backstroke turn	———	———	———
backstroke spin turn	———	———	———
breaststroke turn	———	———	———
breaststroke turn with pull-out	———	———	———
crawl stroke turn	———	———	———
crawl stroke flip turn	———	———	———
elementary backstroke turn	———	———	———
sidestroke turn	———	———	———
IM turns			
fly-to-back turn	———	———	———
back-to-breast turn	———	———	———
back-to-breast flip turn	———	———	———
breast-to-crawl turn	———	———	———

Continue to work in the pool on improving your weaknesses. Set some long-term goals for skill improvement and tailor your fitness swimming workouts to help you reach those goals. Use this checklist once or twice a year to chart your progress.

CHAPTER SEVEN
Standard Workouts

TRAINING METHODS

CONTINUOUS SWIMMING

Oone method of training is to swim continuously for the entire exercise period. Fitness swimmers might swim the same stroke for the entire workout, or they might keep moving by swimming a medley of several different strokes in a definite or random pattern. The two primary variations of continuous swimming are as follows:

1. Swim a predetermined distance.
    a. Swim different distances (longer or shorter) on different days.
    b. Try to maintain or improve your speed (time) over the same distance.
2. Swim as far as possible for a predetermined time period.
    a. Swim different amounts of time (longer or shorter) on different days.
    b. Try to maintain or improve the distance that can be completed in a specific time period.
    c. For a relaxing workout, do not count lengths as you swim for a specific time period. Simply keep moving at a moderate pace for the entire time.

The swimmer must count lengths (from one side to the other side) to keep track of the distance. The following chart provides sample conversions from lengths to yards in a 25-yard pool:

Lengths/Yards	Lengths/Yards	Lengths/Yards	Lengths/Yards
1 = 25	28 = 700	56 = 1,400	80 = 2,000
4 = 100	32 = 800	60 = 1,500	84 = 2,100
8 = 200	36 = 900	64 = 1,600	88 = 2,200
12 = 300	40 = 1,000	68 = 1,700	92 = 2,300
16 = 400	44 = 1,100	70 = 1,750	96 = 2,400
20 = 500	48 = 1,200	72 = 1,800	100 = 2,500
24 = 600	52 = 1,300	76 = 1,900	

Since workouts may be expressed in yards, it is important to learn how to convert yards to lengths and vice versa. This conversion may seem difficult at first, but after a while the conversions become almost automatic as you remember some of the key distances on the chart and work from there to figure out other distances. The standard is that 1 length = 25 yards. Multiply the number of lengths by 25 to convert from lengths to yards (for example, 10 lengths × 25 = 250 yards), or divide the number of yards by 25 to convert from yards to lengths (for example, 1,500 yards ÷ 25 = 60 lengths). Also, many swimmers use ratios, such a 4 lengths per 100 yards, to set up proportions to calculate yards or lengths.

We use the "nearest multiple" to calculate 1/4-mile increments:

18 lengths = 1/4 mile, or 450 yards (actually 10 yds. more than 440 yds.)
35 lengths = 1/2 mile, or 875 yards (actually 5 yds. less than 880 yds.)
53 lengths = 3/4 mile, or 1,325 yds. (actually 5 yds. more than 1,320 yds.)
70 lengths = 1 mile, or 1,750 yds. (actually 10 yds. less than 1,760 yds.)

Many fitness swimmers use a count of 36 lengths for a 1/2-mile swim, 54 lengths for a 3/4 mile swim, and 72 lengths for a 1-mile swim in order to start and finish at the same end of the pool, or to ensure going past the actual distance. A "lap" equals 2 lengths, and a few swimmers keep track of their distances by counting round trips instead of lengths.

It is possible to construct an inexpensive lap counter made of sewing spools on a thin dowel (92, p. 16), moving one spool after each round-trip swim (2 lengths). Some people place coins on the pool side, and move them to keep track of their count (82). You can also check your count on a clicking-type of adding device such as you might use in a grocery store. Most swimmers simply keep track of the distance in their mind as they swim. I find it helpful to use an ascending count for each length, repeating mentally "this is 1 [or 2, or 15, or whatever length number]" during each push-off and several times across the pool for each length. If a mistake is made and the count is lost, the swimmer can make a "best guess" and continue swimming, or go back to whatever length number is remembered and continue from that point.

INTERVAL TRAINING (REPEAT SWIMMING)

Interval training is a method of training that repeatedly alternates periods of swimming with periods of resting. Each of the repeat swims can be done faster than would be possible in a single long-distance swim because the rest periods between each repeat permit the muscular, cardiovascular, and energy-supplying systems of the body to recover to a more normal state before repeating the swim. This method has a long and successful history of use, first in track and then in swimming.

According to Counsilman (*44*, p. 205), the four basic variables of interval training are as follows:

1. Distance—the actual distance of each repeat swim; for example: 25, 50, 75, 100, 200, 400, or 500 yards, or whatever distance you select to swim repetitively.

2. Interval—the amount of rest between each repeat swim; for example: 1-minute rests between 100-yard repeats, 30-second rests between 50-yard repeats, or 15-second rests between 25-yard repeats, or whatever rest period permits you to maintain your speed for all of the repeat swims specified.

3. Repetitions—the actual number of repeat swims for each distance; for example: 15 × 100 yards, 10 × 50 yards, 8 × 25 yards, or whatever *number* of repeats is desired.

4. Time—the actual speed of each repeat swim; sometimes called the intensity of each swim. Usually the idea is to maintain a certain pace for each of the repeat swims; for example: repeating 10 × 100 yards keeping each 100-yard swim at 1:10 or better, 8 × 50 yards keeping each 50-yard swim at 40 seconds or better, or 5 × 25 yards keeping each 25-yard swim at 15 seconds or better, or whatever time is desired for each repeat.

By altering any of these four variables, fitness swimmers can continually challenge themselves with new and different interval workouts.

During the rest periods, fitness swimmers usually just stand up or hang onto the side of the pool. Some coaches advocate slow swimming, or walking or easy jogging in the pool, during the recovery period. It is important to breathe deeply during the rest period, particularly at its beginning, to promote oxygenation of body tissues and removal of fatigue products (carbon dioxide and lactic acid) from the lungs, blood vessels, and muscles. There are several standard methods of deciding the length of the rest periods:

1. Rest a certain amount of time between each repeat. For example, rest 1 minute or 45 or 35 seconds between 100-yard repeats; or rest 40, 30, or 20 seconds between 50-yard repeats; or rest 20, 15, or 5 seconds between 25-yard repeats. Rest whatever time period is suitable for you to maintain your pace for the entire set of repeats. This method tends to work best for beginners who are just learning how to use the pace clock.

2. Start each repeat on a certain time interval. For example, if you were doing 100-yard repeats on 2½ minutes, and it took you 1:35 to swim the distance, you would then have 55 seconds rest (2:30 minus 1:35) before beginning the next repeat. If you were doing 50-yard repeats on 1 minute, and it took you 42 seconds to swim the

distance, you would then have 18 seconds rest (60 seconds minus 42 seconds) before beginning the next repeat. If you were doing 25-yard repeats on 25 seconds, and it took you 16 seconds to swim the distance, you would then have 9 seconds rest (25 seconds minus 16 seconds) before beginning the next repeat. Start each repeat on whatever time interval is suitable for you to maintain your pace for the entire set of repeats. This method tends to work well for more experienced swimmers who are comfortable using the pace clock.

3. Check your heart rate drop-off. A vigorous repeat swim might elevate the heart rate up to 160–180 beats per minute. During the rest period, continually check your heart rate by counting it (for 6 seconds × 10), and when it drops to 100–120 beats per minute, begin the next repeat. Although this method is very beneficial and accurate from a physiological viewpoint, many swimmers prefer to use one of the first two methods to avoid the inconvenience of having to check the heart rate so frequently.

All fitness swimmers who use interval training should experiment by varying their rest periods for their standard repeat swims. Occasionally, the swimmer will repeat using ascending rests (each rest period a little longer) or descending rests (each rest period a little shorter). There is a tendency in competitive swim training to do repeats with an extremely short rest period, perhaps only 3–5 seconds. Occasionally this is good, but there is no true physiological recovery in just a few seconds of rest and the workouts tend to become simply one long continuous swim. The main emphasis in interval training is on the alternation of swimming and resting, with the rest period of sufficient length that the swimmer's heart rate can recover enough to maintain the same pace (same speed or time) on the repeat swims.

BEFORE AND AFTER YOU SWIM

WARM-UP

Warming up prior to fitness swimming is important because it prepares your heart and lungs for greater effort and reduces the chance for muscle and joint injuries to occur (76, p. 27). James Barnard studied the occurrence of sudden death from heart attacks after participation in vigorous sprint (running) activities; his results seem to apply to swimming as well. He found that blood flow through the heart may be interrupted briefly when you start to sprint, and that this short period of inadequate oxygen supply (ischemia) is not related to age or physical condition. He concluded that "warm-up performed immediately before or 10–15 minutes prior to the sudden burst of high-intensity exercise can eliminate or reduce the ischemic response." (23, p. 837)

A "general" warm-up usually consists of stretching and flexibility exercises. Some of my favorite exercises are listed here, and you're encouraged to use these and/or to develop your own favorites.

1. Circle your arm backward, as if doing a one-arm backstroke. Repeat for the other arm.

2. Circle your arm forward, as if doing a one-arm crawl stroke. Repeat for the other arm.

3. Swing your arms from side to side parallel to the ground, crossing them in front of your body and stretching them back as far as possible behind your body.

4. Join your hands over your head with your elbows bent and with your arms just behind your head. Move both arms to the right as far as possible, and then stretch back to the left side as far as possible.

5. Do some deep knee bends slowly and smoothly.

6. Stand on your left foot, bend the other knee and grasp your right foot behind you with your right hand. Pull your foot back as you bend forward very slightly to stretch the front of your leg. Repeat for the other leg. You may have to brace yourself against a wall with your free hand to keep your balance. Do this two or three times for each leg for 5–10 seconds each time.

7. With your feet separated, bend forward and reach down as far as possible toward your toes. Reach both hands out beyond your left foot and stretch, and then out beyond your right foot and stretch before standing up again.

8. Stand about 5 feet from a wall and place your hands against the wall at about shoulder level. Lean into the wall with your body straight. Keep your heels on the ground to stretch your calves. Do this two or three times for 5–10 seconds each time.

9. Stand about 5 feet from a wall and place your hands against the wall at about shoulder level. Keep your arms straight, bend forward, and drop your head down lower than your arms. Do this two or three times for 5–10 seconds each time.

10. This exercise requires a handhold 3–4 feet from the ground. If an exercise bar is not mounted at that height, you may be able to do this exercise by grasping the diving board, a door frame, or the pole that holds up the backstroke flags. Grasp the handhold with your arms straight and keep your feet on the ground directly beneath your hands. Move your hips back and down to stretch in a semipike position. Do this two or three times for 5–10 seconds each time.

11. A chinning bar is required for this exercise. Hang from the bar with your hands at shoulder width. Stretch from your hands and arms down through your toes. Sink down between your arms so that your shoulders move up by your ears. Do this two or three times for 5–10 seconds each time.

12. A chinning bar is required for this exercise. Hang from the bar with your hands at shoulder width. Bend your knees and bring them up to your shoulders, and then return to the starting position.

These exercises, if done for one set of 8–12 repetitions each (unless otherwise noted), will provide most fitness swimmers with adequate stretching and flexibility within a 2–5-minute general warm-up. Extremes in flexibility are not needed by most fitness or Masters swimmers. James Counsilman studied young competitive swimmers, and concluded that flexibility had a very low correlation with success in swimming (41). In fact, many programs probably over-emphasize stretching and flexibility exercises, and could spend the time better with more work in the water. Swimmers who suffer from any unusual limitations in flexibility are advised to investigate and use the 3-S system (Scientific Stretching for Sport), an efficient and effective series of flexibility exercises developed by Laurence Holt (68). Also, older fitness and Masters swimmers may want to do more stretching exercises, as joint/muscle flexibility declines greatly with age.

It is best not to begin your workout by swimming as fast as possible right away. You should do several lengths of easy swimming, pulling, and/or kicking in what is known as a "specific" warm-up before you begin to push harder in your workout. Whether or not a warm-up is written into the sample workouts given at the end of this chapter, readers are advised to complete some type of general and specific warm-up before working out hard in the water. Where the sample workouts do not have a warm-up listed, you may add several lengths into the beginning of the workout as a warm-up, or you may simply use the first few lengths of the written workout as the warm-up period before swimming faster.

WARM-DOWN

At the end of your workout, or after a competitive race, you should try to keep swimming and moving at a fairly slow pace in the water for a few minutes. This is commonly called a warm-down, swim-down, cool-down, loosen-down, or easy, and it helps the swimmer's body recover from great effort to a more normal state. The continued mild exercising promotes circulation and removal of the fatigue products accumulated in the muscles, lungs, and bloodstream during the swim.

The warm-down usually takes a specific form of several lengths of easy swimming, pulling, and/or kicking to finish the workout. Some swimmers also like to do a general warm-down by repeating some or all of their stretching and flexibility exercises after they get out of the water. Whether or not a warm-down is written into the sample workouts, readers are advised to complete some type of general and/or specific warm-down after working out hard in the water. Where the workouts do not have a warm-down listed, you may add several lengths into the end of the workout as a warm-down, or you may simply use the last few lengths of the written workout as the warm-down period before getting out of the pool.

SAMPLE WORKOUTS

Sample workouts are presented in three different formats: lap-swimming, timed, and interval. They should not be regarded as absolutes. Fitness swimmers may change and modify specific workouts, or combine the best parts of several different workouts, to construct a workout that meets their own special needs and interests. If the longest workouts are too much, do just one-half, one-third, or one-fourth of each part of the workout or of the entire workout, or spread one long workout over several days for full completion.

Workouts are made up of *sets*, which are line items or definite units that develop each part of the workout. For example, 10 lengths, 12 minutes, and 6 × 50 are all sets used respectively in the lap-swimming, timed, and interval workouts. If the particular way listed to complete a set is not to your liking or ability, change it—substitute something else. If you repeat a workout sometime in the future, you may want to do each set slightly differently. Remember the importance of variety in your training program. As you gain experience, construct your own workouts or personalize each of these workouts to meet your own needs, interests, and abilities, and to create new variations.

Sets are further specified in terms of *subsets*, which are brief explanations of the way in which the set is to be completed. For example, the set of 10 lengths might be done by swimming breaststroke, and could be summarized as "10 lengths—S breast," with 10 lengths being the set and S breast being the subset. The set of 12 minutes could be completed by swimming 4 minutes of back stroke, 4 minutes of breaststroke, and 4 minutes of crawl stroke, and could be summarized as "12 min.—4 back – 4 breast – 4 crawl." The set of 6 × 50 might be completed with two 50-yard pulls, two 50-yard kicks, and two 50-yard swims, and could be summarized as "6 × 50—2 P, 2 K, 2 S."

Some common terms and abbreviations that are used in the sample workouts are explained here:

- descending—   a way of doing a repeat set in which each repeat is swum faster than the one before it.

89

● _____ each stroke in IM Order—   complete [whatever number of repeats is specified] of fly, back, breast, and crawl.

● easy—   another term for warm-up or warm-down, or a "recovery swim" (a slow, easy swim between fast, hard sets or repeats).

● FLEE—   a contraction of the words "fly" and "free" (crawl stroke = *free*style); refers to the systematic alternation (by 25s, or 50s, or 100s) of the butterfly and crawl strokes.

● 4-3-2-1—   a set of 10 repeats which are completed as follows: 4 at a moderate even pace, 3 at a faster even pace, 2 at a faster even pace, 1 at the fastest possible pace.

● hypoxic—   operating with less oxygen than normal. There are two basic variations: (1) short, fast sprints while holding your breath, or (2) reducing the normal breathing cycle during a longer swim so that you breathe every fifth, seventh, or ninth stroke. This is extremely vigorous training which should not be overdone nor preceded by repeated hyperventilation.

● IM—   individual medley, which consists of the butterfly, back, breast, and crawl strokes in that order; a good all-around test of swimming ability and a way to practice all four competitive strokes in one swim.

● K—   kicking, or practicing the foot and leg actions; may be done with or without a kickboard and with or without swim fins.

● locomotives—   a pattern of swimming a distance in which the pace improves progressively throughout the swim (sometimes also called buildups); for example, a 300 yard swim with the first 100 easy, the second 100 medium, and the last 100 fast; or a 400-yard swim with each 100 faster.

● mixer—   a long medley swim in which the fitness swimmer does some pulling, kicking, and swimming, changing strokes frequently but in random patterns.

● mixer by _____s—   each section of a mixer swim is completed in a different fashion; for example, "1 × 1,000 S— mixer by 100s" means swim 1,000 yards with each of the ten 100s done differently; "1 × 400 S—mixer by 50s" means swim 400 yards with something different for each 50-yard segment of the 400. Any distance may be specified, and the fitness swimmer is challenged to try completely different things for each part of the swim.

● modified IM— for fitness swimmers who have great difficulty with the butterfly stroke, the IM may be modified to crawl – back – breast – crawl; in other words, substitute crawl for fly.

● negative split— swimming any distance so that the second half of the swim is faster than the first half.

● P— pulling, or using a pull buoy to practice the hand and arm strokes; may be done with or without hand paddles.

● pull a partner— swim while dragging another swimmer behind you; the other swimmer holds your ankles and kicks a little. One or both partners may use a pull buoy, and longer "trains" of three or four swimmers can be created.

● reverse IM— a variation changing the IM order to crawl-breast-back-butterfly.

● R-L— one-arm swimming in which the swimmer uses the *Right* arm only down the pool and the *Left* arm only back; may be used for any of the strokes.

● S— swimming in which the whole stroke (pulling and kicking combined) is practiced; if not specified in the subset, S is intended.

● sequences— can be developed (1) for each length of whatever repeat distance is being used; for example, 75s can be swum as "P–K–S" which means pull a length, kick a length, and swim a length; 125s can be swum as "P–K–jog–K–S" which means pull a length, kick a length, water jog a length, kick a length, and swim a length; 50s can be swum as "fly–back" or "breast-crawl," which means one stroke across and another stroke back as specified; or (2) for an entire workout; for example, a 1,075-yard workout could be written in this way: "400-300-200-100-50-25," meaning one repeat of each distance, with the swimmer choosing how to complete that distance (P,K,S,jog, or IM, etc.). Swimmers need to rest an appropriate amount between distances and to adjust their speed for the different distances to be swum.

- sprint— swim as fast as possible, or as close to 100 percent effort as possible, for whatever distance is specified.

- stroke— any stroke *except* crawl stroke: fly, back, breast, elementary back, and side strokes.

- stroke mixer— a long medley swim using several strokes but no crawl stroke, changing strokes often but in no particular order.

- 250 IM— a 10-length or 250-yard swim as follows: 1 length fly–2 lengths back–3 lengths breast–4 lengths crawl.

- water jogging— jogging in waist-deep water (see Chapter 8); if it's impossible to do this because of the depth of the pool, fitness swimmers should substitute something else to complete the set, such as kicking.

The sample workouts use the terms and abbreviations defined here as well as other notations that are self-explanatory. Some of the sample workouts have a *balanced* emphasis, featuring several different strokes or drills within the workout. Other workouts have a *focused* emphasis, concentrating on one particular stroke or procedure throughout the workout. A few workouts are *in between* these two extremes, perhaps varying a focused emphasis periodically in the workout with something different but not enough to create a truly balanced effect. As you study the sample workouts, try to identify each workout according to its emphasis.

When you prepare your own workouts, you must answer the following questions:

- Which method of training will you use: continuous swimming or repeat swimming?
- Which workout format will you use: lap-swimming, timed, or interval?
- How much time do you have to plan your workout?
- What symbols should you use to write down the workout?
- What total distance or total time period do you wish to complete?
- Which workout emphasis will you use: balanced, focused, or in between?

- What will be the composition of the sets and subsets?
- How much will you warm up before and how much will you warm down after your workout?
- How much will you work on your strengths, and how much on your weaknesses?

LAP SWIMMING WORKOUTS

This section contains 41 lap swimming workouts ranging from 20 to 100 lengths. The numbers in the subsets refer to lengths. For example: "15 lengths—5 back – 5 breast – 5 crawl" means swim 5 lengths backstroke, then 5 lengths breaststroke, and finally 5 lengths crawl. The dashes (–) tie the different sections together into one continuous 15-length swim, changing strokes as specified. The symbol "..." means that the pattern listed repeats itself continuously throughout the set or repeats itself as far as possible given the limits of the pattern itself and the total length of the set.

It is recommended that you rest approximately 1 minute between the sets of the workout. A few swimmers may reduce this rest period between sets, making the total workout nearly or completely continuous. Others will need to rest longer than 1 minute before moving into the next set.

Once you are experienced, it may become easy for you to swim through these workouts slowly. Periodically, you'll need to check your heart rate and your speed, comparing them to previous paces to enable you to maximize exercise benefits from your workout.

---

1. 20 lengths—P crawl

    20 lengths total

---

2. 1 length—easy
    2 lengths—back
    4 lengths—side (right)
    8 lengths—breast
    4 lengths—side (left)
    2 lengths—back
    1 length—easy

    22 lengths total

---

3. 24 lengths—S crawl with every 4th length breast and every 8th length back

    24 lengths total

4. 2 lengths—easy
    4 lengths—crawl
    8 lengths—breast
    12 lengths—8 × 1 length sprint, then 4 easy
    —
    26 lengths total

5. 4 lengths—easy P + K
    22 lengths—7 breast – 7 back – 8 crawl
    2 lengths—easy
    —
    28 lengths total

6. 10 lengths—K
    8 lengths—P
    6 lengths—S
    4 lengths—sprint
    2 lengths—easy
    —
    30 lengths total

7. 32 lengths—S crawl with every 4th length breast
    —
    32 lengths total

8. 8 lengths—crawl
    8 lengths—1 elementary back – 1 back...
    8 lengths—1 fly K – 1 breast S...
    8 lengths—crawl
    2 lengths—easy
    —
    34 lengths total

9. 12 lengths—P crawl with hand paddles
    12 lengths—4 fly K – 4 back K – 4 crawl K
    12 lengths—S crawl
    —
    36 lengths total

10. 3 lengths—easy
    10 lengths—1 K – 1 S...
    5 lengths—5 × 1 length sprint
    20 lengths—P crawl
    —
    38 lengths total

11. 40 lengths—strokes only, no crawl
    —
    40 lengths total

12. 24 lengths—mixer
     12 lengths—fin K, no board: 4 fly – 4 back – 4 crawl
      4 lengths—S crawl fast
      2 lengths—easy
     ___
     42 lengths total

13. 16 lengths—P crawl
      4 lengths—IM
     16 lengths—2 back – 2 breast – 2 crawl...
      4 lengths—IM
      4 lengths—easy
     ___
     44 lengths total

14.   4 lengths—easy
     40 lengths—K mixer
      2 lengths—easy
     ___
     46 lengths total

15. 12 lengths—P crawl
      4 lengths—IM
     12 lengths—fin K: 1 fly – 1 back – 1 crawl...
      4 lengths—IM
     12 lengths—4 slow – 4 medium – 4 fast (all crawl)
      4 lengths—easy
     ___
     48 lengths total

16. 50 lengths—10 crawl – 10 back – 10 crawl – 10 breast – 10 crawl
     ___
     50 lengths total

17.   4 lengths—S
     16 lengths—K
     32 lengths—P
     ___
     52 lengths total

18. 24 lengths—warm-up mixer
     16 lengths—2 P back – 2 P breast – 4 P crawl...
      8 lengths—fin K: 2 fly – 2 back – 2 crawl – 2 fly
      4 lengths—IM
      2 lengths—easy
     ___
     54 lengths total

19. 12 lengths—P crawl with hand paddles
      6 lengths—S fly
     12 lengths—P crawl (R – L . . .)
      6 lengths—S back
     12 lengths—S crawl with alternate side breathing
      6 lengths—S breast
      2 lengths—easy
     ──
     56 lengths total

20. 10 lengths—crawl
      4 lengths—IM
     10 lengths—crawl
      4 lengths—IM
     10 lengths—crawl
      4 lengths—IM
     10 lengths—crawl
      4 lengths—IM
      2 lengths—easy
     ──
     58 lengths total

21. 60 lengths—S crawl with every 10th length alternated fly K, back K, and breast K . . .
     ──
     60 lengths total

22. 24 lengths—crawl
     12 lengths—4 fly – 4 back – 4 breast
     24 lengths—8 P crawl – 8 K crawl – 8 S crawl with flip turns
      2 lengths—easy
     ──
     62 lengths total

23.   4 lengths—P
      8 lengths—breast
     12 lengths—K
     16 lengths—2 crawl – 1 back . . .
     12 lengths—P with paddles
      8 lengths—IM
      4 lengths—P
     ──
     64 lengths total

24. 66 lengths—S crawl for time (time this swim on a clock)
     ──
     66 lengths total

25.   8 lengths
      12 lengths
      16 lengths   do something completely different for each set
      28 lengths
       4 lengths
      ──
      68 lengths total

---

26.   70 lengths—S crawl with every 10th length fly
      ──
      70 lengths total

---

27.   72 lengths—8 crawl – 4 back – 8 crawl – 4 breast...
      ──
      72 lengths total

---

28.   20 lengths—P crawl with hand paddles
       4 lengths—fin K fly
      20 lengths—2 back – 2 breast...
       4 lengths—fin K back
      20 lengths—S crawl
       4 lengths—fin K crawl
       2 lengths—easy
      ──
      74 lengths total

---

29.   12 lengths—warm-up mixer
      32 lengths—8 crawl – 4 IM...
      16 lengths—1 R – 1 L – 2 S...
      12 lengths—12 × 1 length sprint
       4 lengths—easy
      ──
      76 lengths total

---

30.   18 lengths—P
       8 lengths—breast
      16 lengths—crawl
       8 lengths—K
      16 lengths—1 side – 1 elementary back...
       8 lengths—8 × 1 length sprint
       4 lengths—easy
      ──
      78 lengths total

31. 16 lengths—crawl
    4 lengths—back
    16 lengths—crawl
    4 lengths—breast
    16 lengths—crawl
    4 lengths—IM
    16 lengths—crawl
    4 lengths—elementary back
    ―
    80 lengths total

---

32. 80 lengths—crawl
    2 lengths—easy
    ―
    82 lengths total

---

33. 8 lengths—2 P – 2 K – 2 S – 2 P
    16 lengths—fin K
    24 lengths—strokes only, no crawl
    32 lengths—crawl
    4 lengths—easy
    ―
    84 lengths total

---

34. 8 lengths—easy
    48 lengths—S crawl changing breathing pattern every 8 lengths
    24 lengths—strokes only, no crawl
    6 lengths—easy
    ―
    86 lengths total

---

35. 8 lengths—easy
    20 lengths—4 IM – 4 crawl...
    16 lengths—same stroke the whole way
    24 lengths—crawl
    12 lengths—K
    8 lengths—easy
    ―
    88 lengths total

---

36. 30 lengths—P crawl
    15 lengths—fin K
    30 lengths—10 back – 10 breast – 10 crawl
    15 lengths—5 P – 5 K – 5 S easy
    ―
    90 lengths total

37.　15 lengths—P
　　　15 lengths—K
　　　15 lengths—S
　　　15 lengths—P
　　　15 lengths—K
　　　15 lengths—S
　　　 2 lengths—easy
　　　──
　　　92 lengths total

38.　 6 lengths—easy
　　　16 lengths—4 × 1 length sprint – rest 1 minute...
　　　40 lengths—P crawl
　　　 8 lengths—4 × 1 length sprint – rest 1 minute...
　　　20 lengths—4 S – 4 K...
　　　 4 lengths—easy
　　　──
　　　94 lengths total

39.　16 lengths—4 P – 4 K – 4 S – 4 P
　　　48 lengths—crawl
　　　32 lengths—1 P – 1 K – 1 S...
　　　──
　　　96 lengths total

40.　 6 lengths—easy
　　　40 lengths—4 IM – 4 P crawl...
　　　10 lengths—K
　　　40 lengths—S crawl
　　　 2 lengths—easy
　　　──
　　　98 lengths total

41.　 4 lengths
　　　 8 lengths
　　　12 lengths
　　　16 lengths　　　do something completely different for each set
　　　20 lengths
　　　40 lengths
　　　──
　　　100 lengths total

TIMED WORKOUTS

This section contains 41 timed workouts. They increase by 1 minute each, and range from 20 to 60 minutes. The instructions are the same as for the lap swimming workouts except that the numbers in the subsets refer to minutes. For example, "15 minutes—5 back – 5 breast – 5 crawl" means swim 5 minutes backstroke, then 5 minutes breaststroke, and finally 5 minutes crawl. The dashes (-) tie the different sections together into one continuous 15-minute swim, changing strokes as specified. The symbol "..." means that the pattern listed repeats itself continuously throughout the set, or repeats itself as far as possible given the limits of the pattern itself and the total length of the set.

You will need to use a regular wall clock, a pace clock, a wristwatch, or a stopwatch to time your sets, but don't be obsessive about this timing. A few seconds either way won't make much difference. Just get as close to the time period of the set as you can.

---

42. 5 min.
    5 min.   equipment-only workout: use a different piece of
    5 min.   equipment for each 5-minute section
    5 min.
    ──
    20 minutes total

---

43. 7 min.—crawl
    7 min.—back
    7 min.—breast
    ──
    21 minutes total

---

44. 1 min.—easy
    2 min.—back
    3 min.—breast
  10 min.—crawl
    3 min.—back
    2 min.—breast
    1 min.—easy
    ──
    22 minutes total

---

45. 4 min.—easy P + K
  15 min.—S weakest stroke (not crawl)
    4 min.—easy P + K
    ──
    23 minutes total

---

46. 3 min.—easy
  14 min.—1 elementary back - 1 side right - 1 breast - 1 side left...
    7 min.—S crawl: 3 at moderate pace - 3 at faster pace - 1 easy
    ──
    24 minutes total

47.   8 min.—warm-up
       12 min.—Cooper's swim test (see Chapter 8)
        5 min.—warm-down
           ——
       25 minutes total

48.   13 min.—P
       13 min.—K
          ——
       26 minutes total

49.   1 min.—easy
       10 min.—back
        5 min.—crawl
       10 min.—breast
        1 min.—easy
          ——
       27 minutes total

50.   28 min.—S crawl
          ——
       28 minutes total

51.   10 min.—4 easy – 3 faster – 2 faster – 1 fastest
       10 min.—1 back – 1 breast...
        9 min.—3 P – 3 K – 3 easy S
          ——
       29 minutes total

52.   15 min.—P
       10 min.—K
        5 min.—S
          ——
       30 minutes total

53.   12 min.—S crawl
        6 min.—K
       12 min.—S any stroke
        1 min.—easy
          ——
       31 minutes total

54.   4 min.—easy
        8 min.—P crawl R – L...
        8 min.—fin K
        8 min.—strokes only, no crawl
        4 min.—easy
          ——
       32 minutes total

55.   5 min.—easy K + S
       15 min.—1 P – 1 K – 1 S...
       10 min.—1 length sprint – rest 15 seconds...
        3 min.—easy
       —
       33 minutes total

56.   11 min.—favorite stroke (not crawl)
       11 min.—weakest stroke (not crawl)
       11 min.—crawl
        1 min.—easy K
       —
       34 minutes total

57.   10 min.—easy P + K + S
       20 min.—S crawl with every 5th length K
        5 min.—easy
       —
       35 minutes total

58.   8 min.—easy P + K
       12 min.—4 slow – 4 medium – 4 fast
       12 min.—S crawl with flip turns
        4 min.—easy P + K
       —
       36 minutes total

59.   1 min.—easy
        5 min.—P crawl with drag board
       10 min.—fin K
       20 min.—S crawl breathing to weak side
        1 min.—easy
       —
       37 minutes total

60.   1 min.—easy
       12 min.—S crawl with right side breathing only
        6 min.—elementary back
       12 min.—S crawl with left side breathing only
        6 min.—side
        1 min.—easy
       —
       38 minutes total

61.   13 min.—back
       13 min.—breast
       13 min.—crawl
       —
       39 minutes total

62.   10 min.—2 P – 1 K – 1 S...
     10 min.—crawl 1 R – 1 L – 2 S...
     10 min.—2 back – 1 elementary back...
     10 min.—3 at moderate pace – 3 at faster pace – 4 easy
     —
     40 minutes total

63.   4 min.—easy
      8 min.—fin K
     12 min.—P crawl with wrist weights
     16 min.—1 fly – 4 back – 5 breast – 6 crawl
      1 min.—easy
     —
     41 minutes total

64.   16 min.—P crawl with hand paddles
     12 min.—stroke mixer
      8 min.—fin K
      4 min.—S crawl fast
      2 min.—easy
     —
     42 minutes total

65.   2 min.—easy P
     15 min.—S weakest stroke (not crawl)
     10 min.—K
     15 min.—S favorite stroke (not crawl)
      1 min.—easy P
     —
     43 minutes total

66.   4 min.—easy
      6 min.—S back R – L...
      6 min.—S back
      6 min.—S breast R – L...
      6 min.—S breast
      6 min.—S crawl R – L...
      6 min.—S crawl
      4 min.—easy
     —
     44 minutes total

67.   5 min.
    5 min.
    5 min.
    5 min.
    5 min   do something completely different for each 5 minute section
    5 min.
    5 min.
    5 min.
    5 min.
    ——
    45 minutes total

68.   4 min.—easy
    40 min.—10 P – 5 K...
    2 min.—easy
    ——
    46 minutes total

69.   20 min.—P crawl changing breathing pattern every 5 minutes
    15 min.—1 back – 1 breast – 1 side...
    10 min.—IM order...
    2 min.—easy elementary back
    ——
    47 minutes total

70.   3 min.—easy P
    6 min.—K no board, no fins
    12 min.—1 length sprint – rest 20 seconds...
    24 min.—3 crawl – 1 back...
    3 min.—easy S
    ——
    48 minutes total

71.   7 min.—easy P + K + S mixer
    7 min.—1 S – 1 K...
    7 min.—crawl
    7 min.—same stroke the whole time
    7 min.—crawl
    7 min.—1 K – 1 S...
    7 min.—easy P + K + S mixer
    ——
    49 minutes total

72.   5 min.—easy P + K
    20 min.—strokes only, no crawl
    5 min.—S crawl breathing every 5th stroke
    20 min.—P crawl, regular breathing, last 1 minute easy
    ——
    50 minutes total

73. 30 min.—stroke mixer
     15 min.—crawl: 5 slow – 5 medium – 5 fast
      6 min.—easy P + K
     ——
     51 minutes total

74.   5 min.—easy K
     28 min.—P crawl with hand paddles
     14 min.—2 back – 2 breast . . .
      5 min.—easy P
     ——
     52 minutes total

75.   4 min.—easy
      9 min.
      9 min.
      9 min.   do something completely different for each 9 minute section
      9 min.
      9 min.
      4 min.—easy

     53 minutes total

76.   2 min.—easy
     50 min.—20 crawl – 5 stroke . . .
      2 min.—easy
     ——
     54 minutes total

77.   5 min.—easy P
     20 min.—crawl
      5 min.—easy K
     20 min.—crawl
      5 min.—easy S
     ——
     55 minutes total

78.   4 min.—easy K
     20 min.—4 S – 2 P . . .
      8 min.—back
     20 min.—6 breathe right – 6 breathe left – 8 alternate side breathing
      4 min.—easy P
     ——
     56 minutes total

79.　6 min.—fin K
　　12 min.—crawl
　　6 min.—fin K
　　12 min.—stroke mixer
　　6 min.—fin K
　　12 min.—crawl
　　3 min.—easy P
　　——
　　57 minutes total

80.　10 min.—crawl
　　4 min.—IM order...
　　10 min.—crawl
　　4 min.—IM order...
　　10 min.—crawl
　　4 min.—IM order...
　　10 min.—crawl
　　4 min.—IM order...
　　2 min.—easy
　　——
　　58 minutes total

81.　4 min.—easy
　　18 min.—P
　　18 min.—K
　　18 min.—S
　　1 min.—easy
　　——
　　59 minutes total

82.　60 min.—continuous swim
　　——
　　60 minutes total

INTERVAL WORKOUTS

This section contains 42 interval workouts. There are two workouts for each of the 100-yard units, ranging from 500 to 2,500 yards. Before trying these workouts, you should review the section on interval training.

For the sets, the first number is the repetitions and the second number is the distance. If there is no first number listed, "1 ×" is understood. For example, "10 × 50" means to swim 50 yards 10 times with an appropriate rest period between each 50-yard segment. If you're not sure of the distance in lengths, divide that number by 25. In the example given, 50 yards ÷ 25 = 2 lengths for each repeat.

The numbers in the subsets refer to the number of repeats to be completed in a specified way. For example: "15 × 100—5 back, 5 breast, 5 crawl" means to swim 100s (4 lengths each) 15 times with an appropriate rest period between each 100. The first five 100s are swum backstroke, the second five 100s are swum breaststroke, and the last five 100s are swum crawl.

You need a rest period or interval between repeats so you can maintain your pace throughout the set for whatever stroke you're using (remember that your speed will be different for the various strokes). You should also rest a minute or two between sets, although experienced swimmers may rest less and beginners may need a little more rest before beginning the next set. It's easy to knock yourself out by attacking these interval sets too vigorously, with your speed too fast, the intervals too tight, or the rest periods too short.

On the other hand, you can swim each repeat so slowly that you begin to feel like you don't need the rest period before starting the next repeat. The proper pace is faster than your normal distance swimming speed, and you should need the rest period to recover for the next repeat. You must do a lot of experimentation with the intervals and rest periods, and you must become very aware of your speed for different distances. This means the consistent use of some kind of pace clock to time your repeats and your rest periods.

Again, the dashes (–) tie different lengths or distances together into one continuous swim, and the symbol "..." means that the pattern listed repeats itself continuously throughout the set or repeats itself as far as possible.

83.	200 mixer warm-up by 25s	200
	4 × 50 P crawl (R–L)	200
	4 × 25—3 sprint, 1 easy	100
		500 yds.

84.	3 × 100—1 easy, 2 crawl	300
	3 × 50—1 fly, 1 back, 1 breast	150
	3 × 25—2 sprint, 1 easy	75
		525 yds.

85.	1 × 200 P crawl	200
	1 × 200 K (fly – back – fly – crawl – fly – back – fly – crawl)	200
	1 × 200 S (50 crawl – 50 back – 50 breast – 50 crawl)	200
		600 yards

86.	5 × 50 P crawl alternated with	250
	4 × 100 S—1 crawl, 1 back, 1 breast, 1 IM	400
		650 yds.

107

87.	3 × 100—1 P, 1 IM, 1 P	300
	4 × 50—descending: each 50 faster	200
	8 × 25 sprint—last 2 easy	200
		700 yds.

88.	200 K–S warm-up	200
	4 × 100—1 crawl, 1 back, 1 breast, 1 crawl	400
	4 × 25 sprint crawl	100
	50 P crawl warm-down	50
		750 yds.

89.	50 warm-up	50
	4 × 100 crawl	400
	4 × 50—2 back, 2 breast	200
	4 × 25 sprint	100
	50 warm-down	50
		800 yds.

90.	1 × 200 P crawl	200
	1 × 200 K with fins (fly – back – fly – crawl – fly – back – fly – crawl)	200
	1 × 200 P crawl with drag board	200
	1 × 200 S (50 crawl – 50 back – 50 breast – 50 crawl)	200
		800 yds.

91.	100 warm-up	100
	12 × 25—sprint	300
	100 easy	100
	12 × 25—sprint	300
	100 warm-down	100
		900 yds.

92.	5 × 100 P crawl alternated with	500
	4 × 100 fin K	400
		900 yds.

93.	1 × 400 P crawl	400
	8 × 50 S crawl on 1:00	400
	1 × 200 easy stroke mixer	200
		1,000 yds.

94.	1 × 400 P crawl	400
	1 × 300 fin K (50 fly – 50 back – 50 crawl...)	300
	1 × 200 S (back – breast...)	200
	1 × 100 S crawl with flip turns	100
	1 × 50 S warm-down	50
		1,050 yds.
95.	1 × 200 P crawl – warm-up	200
	4 × 100 S—1 crawl, 1 back, 1 breast, 1 crawl	400
	1 × 200 S (back – breast...)	200
	4 × 25 sprint crawl	100
	1 × 200 S warm-down	200
		1,100 yds.
96.	6 × 100 P crawl alternated with	600
	5 × 100 IM S	500
		1,100 yds.
97.	200 P warm-up	200
	6 × 100—2 crawl, 2 breast, 2 crawl	600
	6 × 50—2 breast, 2 breast-crawl, 2 crawl	300
	100 P warm-down	100
		1,200 yds.
98.	9 × 50 P crawl alternated with	450
	8 × 100 S—1 IM, 1 back, 1 breast, 1 crawl...	800
		1,250 yds.
99.	1 × 600 S mixer—warm-up	600
	5 × 100 S crawl on 2:30	500
	200 S warm-down	200
		1,300 yds.
100.	1 × 100 warm-up	100
	8 × 150—something different for each 150	1,200
	1 × 50 warm-down	50
		1,350 yds.
101.	5 × 200 P crawl alternated with	1,000
	4 × 100 IM	400
		1,400 yds.

102.	1 × 200 P crawl	200
	8 × 75—for each 75: P – K – S	600
	1 × 200 P crawl	200
	8 × 25 sprint	200
	1 × 200 P crawl	200
		1,400 yds.

103.	1 × 300 P crawl	300
	1 × 300 S back	300
	1 × 300 fin K (100 fly – 100 back – 100 crawl)	300
	1 × 300 S breast	300
	1 × 300 S crawl	300
		1,500 yds.

104.	5 × 100 P—1 warm-up, 4 crawl	500
	10 × 50—3 P, 3 K, 4 S	500
	20 × 25—4 sets of 5 × 25 each set	500
	1 × 50 easy	50
		1,550 yds.

105.	8 × 200—1 P crawl	1,600 yds.
	1 fin K (fly – back – fly – crawl…)	
	1 modified IM with wrist-weights	
	1 S crawl R–L…	
	1 S elementary back–back…	
	1 fin K (fly – back – fly – crawl…)	
	1 S (50 back–50 breast…)	
	1 S (100 S crawl fast for time – 100 easy)	

106.	3 × 150	450
	6 × 75	450
	9 × 50	450
	12 × 25	300
		1,650 yds.

107.	400 warm-up	400
	2 × 200 stroke	400
	easy 50	50
	4 × 100 crawl	400
	easy 50	50
	4 × 50 stroke locomotives: 1/3 easy–1/3 faster– 1/3 fastest for each 50	200
	easy 50	50
	4 × 25 timed sprints	100
	50 warm-down	50
		1,700 yds.

108.	10 × 100	1,000
	10 × 50	500
	10 × 25	250
		1,750 yds.

109.	500 warm-up	500
	8 × 75 S—for each 75: middle length stroke	600
	10 × 50—alternate 50 fast and 50 easy	500
	4 × 25 sprint	100
	100 warm-down	100
		1,800 yds.

110.	5 × 200	1,000
	5 × 100	500
	5 × 50	250
	5 × 25	125
		1,875 yds.

111.	300 warm-up mixer by 50s	300
	8 × 100—2 crawl, 1 IM...	800
	8 × 50—descend 1-4, 5-8	400
	16 × 25—12 sprint, 4 easy	400
		1,900 yds.

112.	300 warm-up	300
	2 × 200—1 stroke, 1 crawl	400
	6 × 50—descending: each 50 faster	300
	150 easy	150
	4 × 100 stroke	400
	10 × 25 sprint	250
	100 warm-down	100
		1,900 yds.

113.	300 warm-up	300
	3 × 500—descending: each 500 faster	1,500
	200 warm-down	200
		2,000 yds.

114.	300 warm-up	300
	5 × 100—1 crawl, 1 IM...	500
	20 × 50—4 sets of 5 × 50 each set	1,000
	200 warm-down	200
		2,000 yds.

115.	1 × 200 warm-up	200
	4 × 100 crawl	400
	6 × 50 K	300
	1 × 400 stroke	400
	4 × 50 crawl	200
	4 × 100 P	400
	8 × 25 —2 each stroke in IM order with last 2 easy	200
		2,100 yds.

116.	1 × 200 warm-up	200
	10 × 100—4 P, 6 S	1,000
	12 × 50—6 K, 6 S	600
	8 × 25—2 each stroke in IM order	200
	1 × 100—warm-down	100
		2,100 yds.

117.	300 warm-up	300
	3 × 200—1 crawl, 1 IM, 1 stroke	600
	easy 100	100
	6 × 50—descending: 1 & 2 slower, 3 & 4 faster, 5 & 6 fastest	300
	easy 100	100
	4 × 100 stroke	400
	easy 100	100
	8 × 25—4 S with starts, 4 K	200
	100 warm-down	100
		2,200 yds.

118.	150 warm-up	150
	1 × 500 FLEE--alternate fly and crawl by 50s	500
	12 × 75—for each 75: P – K – S	900
	6 × 50 stroke—descend 1-3 and 4-6	300
	12 × 25—3 × 1 each in IM order	300
	100 warm-down	100
		2,250 yds.

119.	3 × 200—1 P, 1 IM, 1 K—warm-up	600
	12 × 100—6 P, 6 S	1,200
	8 × 50—4 K, 4 S	400
	100 warm-down	100
		2,300 yds.

120.	2 × 200—1 P, 1 S warm-up	400
	10 × 100—2 P, 2 K, 6 S	1,000
	12 × 50—4 P, 4 K, 4 S	600
	8 × 25—4 K no boards in IM order, 4 S	200
	1 × 100 warm-down	100
		2,300 yds.

121.	1 × 400 warm-up	400
	8 × 25 sprint stroke	200
	8 × 100—alternate 100 IM and 100 P crawl	800
	8 × 25 sprint stroke	200
	8 × 50—alternate 50 S and 50 K	400
	8 × 25 sprint stroke	200
	1 × 200 warm-down	200
		2,400 yds.

122.	1 × 800 P	800
	1 × 400 K	400
	1 × 800 IM S	800
	1 × 400 easy	400
		2,400 yds.

123.	800 warm-up	800
	8 × 125—for each 125: 1st and 5th lengths stroke	1,000
	easy 200	200
	8 × 50—descend 2-4-6-8, easy 1-3-5-7	400
	100 warm-down	100
		2,500 yds.

124.	5 × 100 P crawl alternated with	500
	4 × 500—1 S crawl	2,000
	1 P R–L-crawl...	2,500 yds.
	1 S 50 back – 50 breast...	
	1 S crawl	

REVIEW

Answer as many questions as you can by yourself, then refer to the chapter text or the Index to find the answers to the rest of the questions.

1. What is the difference between continuous swimming and interval training?

2. What are the main variables in continuous swimming and in interval training?

3. 66 lengths = _____ yards

4. 1,250 yards = _____ lengths

5. A lap = _____ lengths

6. Use _____ procedures prior to exercise, and _____ procedures at the completion of your exercise.

7. How do the terms "general" and "specific" relate to warm-up/warm-down procedures?

8. What are your favorite stretching and flexibility exercises? Do you have any additions to those listed in the text?

9. _____ are line items, or definite units, that develop each part of the workout.

10. _____ are brief explanations of the way in which the set is to be completed.

11. P = _____   K = _____   S = _____

12. IM = I _____ M _____

13. What is the difference between a workout that has a balanced emphasis and one that has a focused emphasis?

14. Lap swimming workouts are based on swimming a certain number of _____, while timed workouts are based on swimming for a certain number of _____.

15. Prepare a brief interval workout using 100s, 50s, and 25s. Specify rest periods for each set.

CHAPTER EIGHT
Workout Variations and Related Activities

This chapter describes activities that can add variety to your workouts and help you reach the goals of your training program.

WATER JOGGING

A unique program of jogging in waist-deep water has been promoted by Michael Castronis, assistant professor of physical education at the University of Georgia. Despite an active life-style as a teacher and coach, several years ago Castronis began to suffer from advanced osteoarthritis involving both knees. He continued his normal exercise activities but the pain became increasingly severe and he developed a limp.

One day, Castronis happened to be in the swimming pool and decided, on impulse, to try some flutter kicking with a kickboard. He felt that this was "the most boring activity" he had ever done and "disgustedly" threw the board onto the pool deck. When he noticed the pace clock on the side of the pool, he decided to try something different before getting out:

Standing in waist deep water I began to run, attempting to simulate a true running style. Trying to run quickly by energetically pumping both legs and arms, I soon noticed a cessation of pain. The water supported a great deal of body weight, therefore relieving weight-bearing pressure on my knees. Stopping after fifteen minutes of strenuous running in the water, and timing heart rate by the pulse of the carotid artery, I found it to be 160 beats per minute.... With this new knowledge and with ready access to the pool, a running schedule in water was started with never the slightest twinge of pain.... The limp has disappeared, the leg can be straightened, and now a deep knee bend can be performed. Best of all, I have now returned to my basketball games and my running with no discomfort. In addition to running a mile and a half a day, seven days a week, however, I am continuing to run in water for ten minutes a day. (31, p. 8)

The basic water jogging workout according to Castronis is to run 625 yards (25 lengths) in 10 minutes. I believe that some water jogging can add

115

variety to fitness swimming programs. Use it as part of a workout; use it as part of a long medley swim, alternating different strokes and water jogging lengths; use it as a warm-up or warm-down; use it as a break between repeat sets; use some slow water jogging in place of stationary rest periods at times; occasionally, use it for the entire workout.

The pool itself is a limiting factor in water jogging; it must have a span of 10–25 yards of shallow water to permit this activity. The water should be about waist-deep for the best effect. After several practices, the water jogger usually adjusts to the pool bottom (which may be slippery) and becomes confident enough to run hard without falling. Boots used by scuba divers may be worn by those who use water jogging extensively to gain better traction on slippery pool bottoms. When running in a group in a circular formation (down one side of a lane line and back along the other side), water joggers should space themselves 8–12 feet apart to reduce the effects of "drafting" (being pulled along in the eddy currents of the runner in front of them).

Castronis has seen his chance discovery benefit several students and athletes with a variety of injuries and problems which responded to water jogging as partial therapy. I participated as a subject in a study by Blanche Evans (52) which indicated that water jogging is vigorous enough to elevate the heart rate to the levels where fitness benefits can occur, and that water jogging at slow speeds is comparable in terms of energy expenditure to faster jogging activity on land.

STROKE DRILLS

It is worthwhile for fitness swimmers to work on their strokes periodically in special sessions on technique. This practice may be structured in the form of eight or ten 25s or 50s, it may be less structured in the form of swimming very slowly and concentrating on technique, or it may be specifically written into the workout. All of the drills listed here are primarily designed to work on a particular stroke in terms of pulling, kicking, swimming, or breathing.

BUTTERFLY

Pull with pull buoy.
Pull with hand paddles.
Pull with fist swimming (hands clenched).
Kick with your hands overhead or by your sides.
Kick underwater or on the surface.
Kick on your front, on your side, or on your back.
Kick with or without swim fins.
Swim with your head up (but avoid this if there is any shoulder pain).

Swim using one arm only.

Swim on your back with the dolphin kick and the double overarm stroke (both arms at the same time).

Swim without breathing—hypoxic.

Try different breathing patterns—every stroke, every second stroke, every third stroke.

BACKSTROKE

Pull with pull buoy.

Pull using one arm only.

Pull using double arm backstroke.

Pull using hand paddles.

Pull a partner who holds your ankles and kicks a little.

Pull with fist swimming (hands clenched).

Kick with your arms by your sides, overhead, out at shoulder level, or straight up in the air.

Kick with your hands behind your back or on top of your head, or with your elbows in by your sides and your hands straight up.

Kick with or without swim fins.

Swim with a definite stopping of each hand by the hip before lifting it into the recovery.

Swim with a definite continuous hand action moving each hand past the hip and swinging up into the recovery in one smooth motion.

BREASTSTROKE

Pull with pull buoy.

Pull with hand paddles.

Pull with fist swimming (hands clenched).

Kick with the hands stretched out in front of the shoulders.

Kick with the hands stretched backward, touching the fingertips to the heels or ankles during each kick.

Kick on the back—inverted breaststroke kick.

Kick while treading water—hold your thumbs up (thus immobilizing hands and arms); try to lift your chest and shoulders above the surface of the water.

Swim using one arm only.

Swim with your head up.

Swim underwater using a series of long hand actions.

Swim with the double pull (breathing every other stroke) and compare to breathing every stroke.

CRAWL STROKE

Pull with pull buoy.

Pull using hand paddles.

Pull using one arm only.

Pull with fist swimming (hands clenched).

Pull a partner who holds your ankles and kicks a little.

Kick with your arms overhead, by your sides, or out at shoulder level.

Kick with your hands behind your back, or with your hands out in front and your head up.

Kick on your side.

Kick with a series of full twists.

Kick on the surface or underwater.

Kick with or without swim fins.

Swim with your head up.

Swim without breathing—hypoxic.

Experiment with breathing patterns—to right side only every stroke or every other stroke; to left side only every stroke or every other stroke; every third stroke to opposite sides; breathe 2 to the right and 2 to the left; breathe 3 to the right and 3 to the left; every fifth stroke to opposite sides.

CONTINUOUS EASY/SPRINT KICKING DRILL

Alternate periods of slow easy kicking with periods of faster sprint kicking. Work for 5–10 minutes total and continually vary the lengths of the sprint period and the easy period (5, 10, 15, 20, 25, or 30 seconds each, or longer). There must be a definite change in speed for whatever time period is used. Each swimmer should keep track of the total distance covered in this drill. Two good variations of the drill are to do the kicking with swim fins on and to do the drill swimming instead of kicking.

INDIVIDUAL MEDLEY PATTERNS

There are three basic IM distances: 100-yard IM (25 fly – 25 back – 25 breast – 25 crawl), 200-yard IM (50 fly – 50 back – 50 breast – 50 crawl), and 400-yard IM (100 fly – 100 back – 100 breast – 100 crawl). Some of the many other sequences that could be created are as follows:

50 IM: ½ length each stroke

__ × 50: __ fly-back, __ back-breast, __ breast-crawl

__ × 50: 1 fly-back, 1 back-breast, 1 breast-crawl, 1 crawl-fly...

8 × 50: fly, fly-back, back, back-breast, breast, breast-crawl, crawl, crawl-fly

75 IM: leave one stroke out

75 stroke IM: fly–back–breast

4 × 100:   1 fly–back–fly–back,
              1 back–breast–back–breast,
              1 breast–crawl–breast–crawl,
              1 crawl–fly–crawl–fly

125: 100 IM + favorite stroke

125: 100 IM + weakest stroke

125 IM: use any one stroke for 2 lengths, with 1 length each for the other three strokes; use IM order

4 × 125:   1 fly–back–breast–crawl–fly,
              1 back–breast–crawl–fly–back,
              1 breast–crawl–fly–back–breast,
              1 crawl–fly–back–breast–crawl

150 IM: leave one stroke out

150: fly–crawl–back–crawl–breast–crawl

150 stroke IM: 50 fly – 50 back – 50 breast

200: 100 IM – 100 IM

200: K–S by stroke in IM order

200: fly–crawl–back–crawl–breast–crawl–choice–crawl

250 IM: 25 fly – 50 back – 75 breast – 100 crawl

250 IM: 100 fly – 75 back – 50 breast – 25 crawl

300 IM: 75 fly – 75 back – 75 breast – 75 crawl

300: 100 IM – 100 IM – 100 IM

400: 100 IM – 100 IM – 100 IM – 100 IM

800 IM: 200 fly – 200 back – 200 breast – 200 crawl

1-mile workout: 150 warm-up – 800 IM – 400 IM – 200 IM –
                    100 IM – 100 warm-down

Reverse IM: change order of strokes to crawl – breast – back – fly

PYRAMIDS

In pyramids, the sets in the workout change in length according to a definite progression. You can pyramid by 25s, 50s, 100s, 200s, etc. The pyramid can go up (for example, 50/100/150/200/250/300 = 1,050 yards or 42 lengths), down (for example, 400/300/200/100 = 1,000 yards or 40 lengths), or up and down (for example, 200/400/600/400/200 = 1,800 yards or 72 lengths). Some interesting sequences or patterns can be set up. Follow these guidelines: (1) adjust your rest periods between each part of the pyramid sequence based upon the adjacent distances and your effort, (2) adjust your speed according to the distance you are completing, and (3) use the same stroke for each of the sets.

WHEEL OF FORTUNE

The original Wheel of Fortune workout was presented by Scott Seely, coach of the Dayton Dolphins, and was designed as a change-of-pace workout for an age-group swimming team (117, p. 27). This workout plan includes 100 possible subsets which are listed consecutively on a large chart. The last two digits of an electronic stopwatch are used to determine what an individual or small group will do. The running time on the digital watch is stopped at the command of a swimmer, and the last two digits on the stopwatch are noted and then checked against the chart of subsets. The swimmer or group must do whatever is called for by the numbers—no changes or substitutions are permitted.

Each swimmer or group can go through the procedure a certain number of times, or for a certain time period. This workout plan is interesting because it contains so many subset variations, and because it introduces the element of chance. The following Wheel of Fortune is based upon my favorite subsets (refer to Chapter 7 for explanation of sets and subsets):

01: 4 × 200 modified IM (50 crawl – 50 back – 50 breast – 50 crawl)
02: 1 × 300 fin K (fly–back–crawl...)
03: 12 × 50 S—4 fly–back, 4 back–breast, 4 breast–crawl
04: 8 × 25 sprint—2 each stroke in IM order
05: Swim 1500 crawl with every 5th length alternated back and breast
06: 10 × 50 S—4 moderate, 3 faster, 2 faster, 1 fastest
07: 2 × 400 S—1 IM, 1 stroke
08: 1 × 200 S crawl—breathe every 5th stroke
09: 600–300–200–100
10: 12 × 25 sprint—3 each stroke in IM order

11: 1 × 1500 P crawl
12: 800–400–200
13: 12 × 100 mixers—something different for each 100
14: 500–400–300–200–100
15: 8 × 50 S backstroke
16: 5 × 100 S—descend 1-3-5, easy P 2-4
17: 1 × 800 build up (easy 300 – medium 300 – fast 200)
18: 10 × 25 sprint—2 crawl, 2 back, 2 crawl, 2 breast, 2 crawl
19: 1 × 400 S (100 IM – 100 IM – 100 IM – 100 IM)
20: 25 × 25—5 sets of 5 × 25 each set

21: 5 × 100—descending: each 100 faster
22: 1 × 400 fin K—no kickboard
23: 3 × 300 locomotives—each 100 faster within continuous 300
24: 10 × 50 S—for each 50: breast across – crawl back
25: 3 × 200—for each 200: easy across – sprint back ...
26: 8 × 50 S—descend 2-4-6-8, easy 1-3-5-7
27: 6 × 150—for each 150: 50 P – 50 K – 50 S
28: 12 × 50 P crawl—for each 50: R–L
29: 1 × 300 P breast
30: 6 × 250 S—for each 250: 25-50-75-100

31: 10 × 75—for each 75: P–K–S
32: 8 × 50—for each 50: K across – S back
33: Swim 800 of your favorite stroke (not crawl)
34: 16 × 25 sprint—4 crawl, 4 back, 4 breast, 4 crawl
35: 100/200/300/400/300/200/100
36: 6 × 50 S—1 and 2 moderate, 3 and 4 faster, 5 and 6 fastest
37: Swim 500 crawl—change breathing pattern every 100
38: 4 × 100 S—for each 100: R–L– crawl–fly
39: 1 × 500 P back
40: 8 × 50 S—alternate 50 fly–back and 50 breast–crawl

41: 3 × 400—1 back, 1 breast, 1 crawl
42: 6 × 100—1 IM, 1 reverse IM ...
43: 12 × 50—alternate 50 stroke and 50 crawl
44: Swim 800 of your weakest stroke (not crawl)
45: 6 × 50 descending—each 50 faster
46: 400 S—alternate 25 elementary back and 25 back ...
47: 8 × 25—start in middle of pool, sprint 1/2 length in and 1/2 length out
48: Swim 1,000 crawl with every 4th length K
49: 10 × 100—2 S, 2 P, 2 K, 2 P, 2 S
50: 10 × 25—start 5 yds. from wall, turn, sprint 1 length

51: Swim as far as possible in 30 minutes
52: 1 × 500 S crawl with flip turns
53: 20 × 50 sprints
54: 3 × 500—1 P, 1 K, 1 S
55: 8 × 75 S—for each 75: middle-length stroke
56: 1 × 400 S crawl with a negative split (2nd 200 faster than 1st)
57: 12 × 50 S—for each 50: any stroke across – different stroke back
58: 1 × 900 S (200 P crawl – 100 S elementary back ...)
59: 16 × 100—1 S back, 1 S breast, 1 fin K, 1 S crawl ...
60: 6 × 50 fist swimming – crawl

121

61: 1 × 800 S crawl with every 4th length back
62: Swim 400 of your favorite stroke (not crawl)
63: 5 × 200—1 back, 1 fly fin K, 1 breast, 1 back fin K, 1 crawl
64: 10 × 100 S alternated with 10 × 50 P crawl
65: 6 × 50 buildups—for each 50: 1st 1/3 easy-2nd 1/3 medium-3rd 1/3 fast
66: 6 × 75 S—for each 75: middle-length fly
67: 1 × 800 S crawl with a negative split (2nd 400 faster than 1st)
68: 6 × 100 fin K—no kickboard
69: 1 × 1,000 mixer—any stroke, any order
70: 3 × 200—1 IM, 1 stroke, 1 crawl

71: 1 × 800 P crawl with hand paddles
72: 5 × 100 P crawl alternated with 4 × 100 IM S
73: Swim 400 of your weakest stroke (not crawl)
74: 6 × 50 S with fins—2 fly, 2 back, 2 crawl
75: 16 × 25—alternate sprint K and sprint S
76: 1 × 800 IM S
77: 1 × 1,000 S crawl for time
78: 1 × 500 P crawl with drag board
79: Swim as far as possible in 20 minutes
80: 4 × 250 IM (25 fly – 50 back – 75 breast – 100 crawl)

81: Swim 1650 crawl for time
82: 1 × 400 P crawl with drag board and hand paddles
83: 8 × 100 S alternated with 8 × 50 K
84: 1 × 300 S crawl with flip turns
85: 10 × 50—alternate fast 50s and easy 50s
86: 4 × 100 IM alternated with 3 × 400 S crawl
87: 3 × 200 descending—each 200 faster
88: 1 × 500 K (100 IM – 100 fly – 100 back – 100 breast – 100 crawl)
89: 8 × 200 mixers—something different for each 200
90: 4 × 150 P crawl with drag board

91: 8 × 100 S breast
92: 10 × 125—for each 125: 50 crawl – 25 stroke – 50 crawl
93: 1 × 1000 S crawl with every 10th length fly
94: 6 × 100 S—1 IM, 1 back, 1 IM, 1 breast, 1 IM, 1 crawl
95: 8 × 50 S—descend 1–4, and descend 5–8
96: Swim 400 crawl—change breathing pattern every 50
97: 5 × 200 S alternated with 5 × 100 P crawl
98: 15 × 100—5 P, 5 K, 5 S
99: 10 × 50 S—1 fly, 3 back, 3 breast, 3 crawl
00: Swim 1 mile (70 lengths) for time

SPECIAL EVENTS

WATER POLO

To play water polo you need goals, hats, a ball, a whistle, enough people for two teams, and a competent official. This game must be played with great restraint in order to avoid injuries—avoid hard contact and extremely aggressive play. Don't turn a change-of-pace workout into "animal ball."

BIATHLON

For those who do some jogging and swimming, the biathlon is an interesting event combining the two fitness activities. A bathing suit, sneakers, running shorts, and tee shirt are worn, and the runners must be prepared to enter the water right after they run. Although any distances can be used, a common procedure is to run 2 miles, then swim 1/2 mile (usually a 4:1 ratio is set up). Timing is continuous from start to finish. Two groups are often used, with everyone having a partner to pick up the time at the end of the run and at the end of the swim, and to count laps. Several maps of the running course are posted so everyone runs the same distance. The running portion can be done on an indoor/outdoor track or planned route, and the swimming portion works well in a pool or an open-water situation (use appropriate safety precautions).

TRIATHLON

The triathlon is similar to the biathlon but combines three fitness activities, swim–bike–run, into one continuous event. There are somewhat short versions of the triathlon; for example, 1-mile swim–30-mile bike ride–10-mile run. On the other hand, the Hawaiian Iron Man Contest consists of a 2.5-mile ocean swim – 112-mile bike ride – 26.2-mile run (full marathon).

To develop interest in the event in our area, we sponsored a greatly scaled-down version called the fitness triathlon. This noncompetitive fitness event consisted of a 1/4-mile swim in a pool – 8-mile bike ride – 3-mile run. Each segment was self-timed for personal evaluation only. Snacks and juice were provided during short breaks between events. This "developmental" format permitted the triathletes to try out the event without jumping right into an incredibly long endurance contest, and reactions from the participants were very positive.

SWIM AND STAY FIT PROGRAM

The American Red Cross sponsors a Swim and Stay Fit program as part of its water safety program.

Swim and Stay Fit is a planned activity to encourage individuals to swim regularly and frequently until 50 or more miles are reached. It should be made clear that the Swim and Stay Fit activity is not a marathon, not a race, not competitive, not an endurance contest. Its goal is to improve the physical fitness of the swimmer, and not in any way to detract from it; it is meant to encourage regular swimming. (2, p. 1)

The program is directed through local Red Cross Chapters by their volunteer water safety committees. Public pools, private pools, residential pools, swim clubs, camps, local schools, colleges, and youth agencies may cooperate in the program by serving as the swimmers' home facilities. Program monitors (usually Red Cross water safety instructors) coordinate swimming activity and record-keeping at each facility, and make sure that each swimmer participates under safe conditions. Anyone who can swim is eligible for the program. Those who have health problems should enroll only after consulting a doctor and notifying the facility supervisors of their special conditions.

The goal of the program is to swim a total of 50 miles. For the first 3 miles, swimmers must complete at least 440 yards during each swim at the facility, although they may stop to rest whenever needed. The remaining distance (47 miles) must be completed with continuous swims in multiples of 1/4 mile, using any stroke(s) preferred. Two hundred 440-yard segments are needed to complete the 50-mile total. Upon completion, the Red Cross hopes the individual will be in "excellent physical condition...[and] motivated to continue a personal program of regular and frequent swimming" (2, p. 4).

Completed distances are recorded on prominently displayed wall charts at the swimmer's home facility. It is possible to receive credit for swimming away from the home facility, provided that distances are verified by the monitor at the other facility on official forms. Unofficial records may be kept by the swimmer on a wallet-sized card issued by the monitor at the start of the program. Wallet-sized certificates are issued to individuals completing each 10-, 20-, 30-, 40-, and 50-mile segment. An attractive pin and emblem can be purchased for a small fee by the individual completing the 50 miles.

OBSERVATION TECHNIQUES

The use of videotape equipment provides the opportunity to view your own strokes, which is usually of great motivational value to fitness swimmers. This equipment has some limitations: it typically can't be taken underwater for the most meaningful view of the strokes; its slow-motion operation is sometimes a little cloudy and tedious (especially in comparison to motion picture film); continuous filming takes at least as long to play back as it did to film; and there is a substantial amount of

124

gadgetry involved. However, the equipment can be used to analyze strokes as seen on the surface. Swimmers can swim in toward the camera (head on), away from the camera (head away), and across the camera's view (profile—both sides).

Swimmers can also watch each other's strokes and turns underwater to observe common mistakes and good examples. Although they can simply hold their breath and use their goggles, the procedure works better with masks and snorkels for everybody. This underwater view of strokes is most significant because this is where propulsion occurs. In general, there is too much surface analysis and too little underwater analysis of strokes and turns.

AEROBIC SWIM TESTS

There are two swimming tests that evaluate your aerobic capacity (the ability of your body to process oxygen and remove fatigue products). After you have been exercising for 2–3 months, you may want to place yourself into a fitness category by using one or both of these tests. Kenneth Cooper cautioned:

> Field testing of physical fitness is no longer a required part of the aerobics program and is in fact contraindicated initially in the deconditioned person over thirty-five years of age. Yet it is an easy way to measure the success of your program and continues to be a popular feature of the aerobics system. It gives you a reliable estimate of your aerobic capacity, or oxygen consumption, yet does not require expensive laboratory equipment. It can be used by people of all ages, and large groups can be tested at one time. (36, p. 87)

Periodically, you may wish to retake the test as a check on your progress and classification, or as a high-intensity part of your total workout.

12-Minute Swim Test

The objective of Cooper's swim test is to swim as far as possible in 12 minutes. It's best to have someone else time you, but you can time yourself if necessary on a large, visible pace clock (manual or digital), or on your own watch (on your wrist if it's waterproof, or attached to the starting block, or left within reach on the poolside). You may switch or mix strokes in any way, but crawl stroke will be the best and fastest choice for most people. No equipment can be used during the test. You may stop to rest if necessary during the test, but it's better to keep moving since a stop will have a negative effect on your score. Most swimmers will use an ascending count to keep track of their lengths.

The norms (35, p. 142) for men and women of all age groups are presented in Table 8-1. However, this test does not take into account your own "starting point" in fitness swimming or how long and how frequently you've been participating, factors that could have a major impact on your score. Questions can be raised about the factors that are actually measured (swimming speed, technique, cardiovascular endurance, experience, sense of pace, ability in breathing, turning ability, etc.), the source of the norms, the size of the sample population originally tested, and how extensive the testing was in each age group. Therefore, this test should be used with some caution by fitness swimmers. I have seen some swimmers become very discouraged when the test places them in a low fitness category after they have worked hard in the water for several weeks or months. Fitness swimmers must put the test results (whether good or bad) in perspective, and instructors must interpret the results in light of the many variables that are involved in this kind of swimming experience.

TABLE 8-1. Norms for 12-Minute Swim Test (distances in yards)

Fitness category		Age Group					
		13–19	20–29	30–39	40–49	50–59	60+
I. Very poor	(men)	<500	<400	<350	<300	<250	<250
	(women)	<400	<300	<250	<200	<150	<150
II. Poor	(men)	500–599	400–499	350–449	300–399	250–349	250–299
	(women)	400–499	300–399	250–349	200–299	150–249	150–199
III. Fair	(men)	600–699	500–599	450–549	400–499	350–449	300–399
	(women)	500–599	400–499	350–449	300–399	250–349	200–299
IV. Good	(men)	700–799	600–699	550–649	500–599	450–549	400–499
	(women)	600–699	500–599	450–549	400–499	350–449	300–399
V. Excellent	(men)	>800	>700	>650	>600	>550	>500
	(women)	>700	>600	>550	>500	>450	>400

Note: The symbol < means "less than" and the symbol > means "more than."

From *The Aerobics Program For Total Well-Being* by Dr. Kenneth H. Cooper © 1982 by Kenneth H. Cooper. Reprinted by permission of the publisher, M. Evans and Co., Inc., New York, N.Y. 10017.

Every time you take the test, you will learn how to take the test better. One trial is not sufficient for the best assessment of your fitness level. My recommendation is to take this test from time to time and to compare your scores, which should show a pattern of improvement. Use the test as a brief, intense workout, but don't get too elated if you score high or too depressed if you score low. Be careful about generalizing the results of this test to your overall "fitness"—even the experts have trouble defining that term in fine detail ("fitness is whatever the particular test says it is"). Your results are simply your score on this particular test, one of many evaluative tests or challenges that you could have selected for yourself. Many different factors contribute to your general level of fitness, and your frequent, vigorous participation is far more important than your score on a 12-minute swim test.

24-Minute Swim Test

The objective of the Hutinger swim test is to swim as far as possible in 24 minutes. The test was devised "to enable master swimmers to evaluate their performance more specifically. It is especially useful for the swimmer who has not achieved the top ten ratings [national rankings in each event] and wishes to determine his fitness level" (*77*, p. 20). Swimmers should follow the instructions given for Cooper's swim test, except for the time.

Norms (*77*, p. 20) for men and women of all age groups are presented in Table 8-2, and the same interpretive comments apply to this test as to the 12-minute test. Also, remember that this test is intended for Masters Swimmers, or those who are involved with adult age-group competition. Regular fitness swimmers are at a slight disadvantage because the test was not designed for them. If you can keep some of the previously stated cautions in mind, this test will be a good workout for you and a real challenge in terms of improving your distance.

TABLE 8-2. Norms for Hutinger's Swim Test (distances in yards)

Rating	Age Group				
(Men)	20–30	31–40	41–50	51–60	61 and over
Champion	2,000	1,900	1,750	1,650	1,550
Excellent	1,650	1,550	1,400	1,300	1,200
Good	1,200	1,100	1,000	900	800
Fair	800	750	700	650	600
Poor	600	550	500	450	400
(Women)					
Champion	1,850	1,750	1,650	1,500	1,450
Excellent	1,500	1,400	1,300	1,200	1,100
Good	1,100	1,000	900	800	700
Fair	700	650	600	550	500
Poor	500	450	400	350	300

Note: Reprinted by permission of Paul Hutinger, "Aerobic Capacities," *Aquatic World* (January 1976): 20.

REVIEW

Answer as many questions as you can by yourself, then refer to the chapter text or the Index to find the answers to the rest of the questions.

1. Running in waist-deep water is called _____.
2. Select one new drill for each stroke to help you develop your skill and technique: fly, back, breast, crawl.
3. Select a workout from the Wheel of Fortune. Which sets did you receive?

4. An event which combines running and swimming is called a _____.

5. Which fitness category are you in, based on Cooper's 12-minute Swim Test?

6. Why is it important to know your "starting point" when evaluating your test results on the 12-minute Swim Test?

7. Have you tried any of the workout variations or other procedures that have been presented? Which ones?

CHAPTER NINE
The Masters Swimming Program

Paul Hutinger called lifelong exercise an anti-aging pill, because the physical condition of older people with a long history of exercise can, in some ways, be as good as that of much younger people. He believed that several factors of aging—tissue condition (anatomical), functional ability (physiological), and intellectual capacity (psychological)—can be improved by vigorous exercise, with the result that individuals can perform, look, and feel younger than their actual age (78, p. 18). The Masters Swimming Program is a good way of reaching that goal.

Masters Swimming is a program of swimming for fitness which features age-group competition for adults. Each swimmer is motivated by a desire for better health and/or better performances, and the program tries to strike a balance between training for health purposes and for competitive goals. According to the Masters Swim Committee:

> The Masters Swim Program is designed as a fun and physical fitness program to encourage adults . . . to swim regularly to gain the many important physical and mental health benefits. Among those benefits are: improved cardiovascular and respiratory efficiency—help in preventing coronary disease—lower blood pressure—relief from the normal tensions accumulated during the day—improved muscle tone, and general physical appearance and posture—aid in weight reduction and control programs. (94, p. 3)

HISTORY AND STRUCTURE

Dr. Ransom J. Arthur originated the idea of Masters Swimming. While an officer in the Navy Medical Corps, Dr. Arthur coached Navy teams of various ages for many years and developed the concept of a continuing program for adults which emphasized training for health reasons, with competition as an added incentive or benefit (18, 20).

John Spannuth, who was at that time the Director of the Amarillo (Texas) Aquatic Club and the President of the American Swim Coaches Association, became interested in the idea and hosted the first National

Masters Championships in Amarillo in May 1970 (5, p. 36). This 4-day meet attracted approximately 50 swimmers, who subsequently went home and loosely organized Masters Swimming on a local, state, and regional basis.

Masters Swimming became part of the National American Athletic Union (AAU) Aquatics Program at the 1971 AAU Annual Meeting at Lake Placid, New York (6, p. 23). In 1980, as a part of the massive reorganization of sports administration in the country, the Masters Program formed its own independent organization, the Masters Swimming Corporation (17, p. 87). By 1982, the Masters Program had settled under the auspices of U.S. Masters Swimming, Inc. (USMS).

A parallel program has developed within the YMCAs, and the first National Invitational YMCA Masters Championships were held in 1976 at the Reading (Pennsylvania) YMCA. This meet has grown over the years, and the rules and regulations governing YMCA Masters competition were adopted in April 1979.

> Masters swimming should be regarded as a vast physical conditioning program fitting into the modern YMCA concept of physical fitness for adults. Its objective should be to improve health and maintain it via participation in a long term program of regularly scheduled swimming and conditioning activities. (49, p. 2)

Many Masters swimmers now participate in both the USMS and YMCA programs. It is to be hoped that these programs will continue to complement and strengthen each other, increasing the opportunities for training and competition for Masters swimmers.

COMPETITION PROCEDURES

ELIGIBILITY

Anyone who is 25 years of age or older is eligible to compete in Masters Swimming. There are no exceptions—even coaches, trainers, former collegiate All-Americans, former world record holders, and professional marathoners are eligible. However, once declared and registered as a Masters Swimmer, the athlete is no longer eligible to compete in the Unrestricted Amateur Division with the younger swimmers.

Masters swimmers compete in officially recognized age groups of 5-year intervals: 25–29, 30–34, 35–39, 40–44, 45–49, 50–54, 55–59, 60–64, 65–69, 70–74, 75–79, 80–84, 85–89, and 90 and older. There is also an unofficial group for 20–24-year-olds.

LOCAL MEETS

For local meets competitors submit seed times for the events they want to enter by the entry deadline. A seed time is a swimmer's best previous time in a particular event. For example, if 31.1 seconds is your best time for the 50-yard freestyle event, you submit 31.1 seconds as your seed time so that you will be placed in a lane near swimmers of comparable speed. If you've never swum an event before, you submit "N.T." or "No Time," which indicates no previous time in that event.

A small fee is paid in advance for each event to cover meet expenses, awards, and refreshments. Late entries ("deck entries") are permitted, but a higher fee is charged. Relays (four-person teams) are organized in 10-year age groups, determined by the age of the youngest member of the relay. The 10-year age span promotes greater participation in relay events by providing a larger number of swimmers to draw from to create the relay teams. Team scores are kept, with relay places counting double the value of a comparable individual place in an event. Awards are presented, and a social follows the meet.

Competitors swim each event in heats, which are set up on the basis of the previously submitted seed times. For example, if 17 swimmers entered the 200–yard breaststroke event in a 6-lane pool, they would be seeded into three heats as follows: first heat—5 slowest swimmers, second heat—next 6 faster swimmers, and third heat—6 fastest swimmers. Within each heat, the swimmers are assigned to lanes as follows: the fastest seed time swims in lane 3, the next fastest in lane 4, the next in lane 2, the next in lane 5, the next in lane 1, and the slowest in lane 6. Since swimmers are assigned to heats on the basis of seed time, men and women, and all different age groups, might swim together in one heat.

When all competitors have swum the event, the swimmers' times are handed in to the scorer's table. The scorekeeper then takes the actual performance times from the event and reorganizes these times into the appropriate age groups for men and women to prepare the final results for that particular event.

A meet might offer the following events:

1. 200-yd. Free Relay (four swimmers, each swimming 50 yards; free or freestyle means any stroke, but most swimmers will use the crawl stroke because it is the fastest stroke)
2. 500-yd. Free
3. 100-yd. Back
4. 50-yd. Fly
5. 200-yd. Breast
6. 100-yd. Free
7. 50-yd. Back
8. 200-yd. Fly
9. 200-yd. IM
10. 100-yd. Breast
11. 50-yd. Free
12. 200-yd. Back

13. 100-yd. Fly
14. 50-yd. Breast
15. 200-yd. Free
16. 100-yd. IM
17. 200-yd. Medley Relay (four swimmers, each swimming 50 yards; first swims backstroke, second swims breaststroke, third swims butterfly stroke, and fourth swims freestyle or crawl stroke)
18. 200-yd. Mixed Free Relay (four swimmers, each swimming 50 yards crawl stroke; "mixed" refers to a relay team consisting of two men and two women)

Other meets might offer the same events but in a different order, and still others might eliminate some of the shorter events and feature longer events, such as the 400-yd. IM, 1,000-yd, or 1,650 yd. Free, 400-yd. Relays, and 800-yd. Free Relay. Much depends on the ability and experience of the hosts and the expected competitors, but all feature something for everyone who wants to participate.

NATIONAL COMPETITION

Competition has been provided in the National Masters Championships since 1970 (*13, 18, 20*). Usually, two Nationals are held: short-course (in a 25-yard pool), and long-course (in a 50-meter pool). The National Championships are held with a 3-day or 4-day format. For example, the 1978 National Championship in San Antonio, Texas, (short-course) had the following schedule of events:

FRIDAY, MAY *19, 10:00* A.M.   WARM-UP 8:30 A.M.

1	Women's	200 yd.	Backstroke
2	Men's	200 yd.	Backstroke
3	Women's	50 yd.	Freestyle
4	Men's	50 yd.	Freestyle
5	Women's	200 yd.	Breaststroke
6	Men's	200 yd.	Breaststroke
7	Women's	100 yd.	Individual Medley
8	Men's	100 yd.	Individual Medley
9	Women's	200 yd.	Free Relay
10	Men's	200 yd.	Free Relay

SATURDAY, MAY *20, 10:00* A.M.   WARM-UP 8:30 A.M.

11	Women's	200 yd.	Individual Medley
12	Men's	200 yd.	Individual Medley
13	Women's	50 yd.	Butterfly
14	Men's	50 yd.	Butterfly
15	Women's	100 yd.	Breaststroke
16	Men's	100 yd.	Breaststroke

17	Women's	500 yd.	Freestyle
18	Men's	500 yd.	Freestyle
19	Women's	200 yd.	Medley Relay
20	Men's	200 yd.	Medley Relay

SUNDAY, MAY 21, 10:00 A.M.   WARM-UP 8:30 A.M.

21	Women's	200 yd.	Freestyle
22	Men's	200 yd.	Freestyle
23	Women's	100 yd.	Butterfly
24	Men's	100 yd.	Butterfly
25	Women's	100 yd.	Backstroke
26	Men's	100 yd.	Backstroke
27	Women's	100 yd.	Freestyle
28	Men's	100 yd.	Freestyle
29	Mixed	200 yd.	Free Relay

MONDAY, MAY 22, 10:00 A.M.   WARM-UP 8:30 A.M.

30	Men's	1,650 yd.	Freestyle
31	Women's	1,650 yd.	Freestyle

There are some restrictions on the number of events that each swimmer can enter. In the 1977 National Championship at Spokane, for example, competitors could enter seven events but only swim a maximum of five individual events, with no more than three individual events per day. Swimmers were permitted to enter only one freestyle relay, one medley relay, and one mixed freestyle relay in this particular meet.

At the present time, there are no "qualifying times" for Nationals, so anyone may enter regardless of speed. All-American honors are awarded to the person who swims the best time in an event anywhere in the United States for the calendar year. A 5-year participation patch is given to those who participate in one or both Nationals for 5 consecutive years.

INTERNATIONAL COMPETITION

In addition to the United States, several other countries participate in Masters Swimming, including the United Kingdom, Australia, New Zealand, Japan, Germany, Sweden, and Finland (18, and 20). Team trips have been made abroad, with dual meet competition in the host country. The first "World Championship" meet was held in Toronto, Canada, in August 1978 and attracted swimmers from many different countries. The U.S. National Masters Championships usually have a number of foreign entries.

OPEN WATER COMPETITION

Masters competition in open water swimming is growing in popularity. Many swimmers enjoy the freedom from the usual closed course in a swimming pool (no lane lines, no walls, no turns, etc.). The emphasis on long distances and on the swimmer's stamina/endurance is quite different than the usual short events in most Masters swimming meets. Some Masters swimmers who would be regarded as slow in the standard events may actually find that they can excel in the longer open water situation.

The rules for these events are typically brief. For example, at the Ocean City (New Jersey) Lifeguard Association Masters Ocean Swim on July 31, 1982, a map of the swim course was given to participants along with the following instructions:

1. All contestants must start and finish within the designated areas.
2. All contestants must swim on the seaward side of all flags. Any swimmer who "cuts" the first or last double flag will be disqualified.
3. Any contestant who drops out of the swim must notify either an escort boat or the beach patrol heandquarters at 12th St. Beach.

GUIDELINES FOR PARTICIPANTS

COMPETITIVE GROUPINGS

Masters swimmers enter the meets that are available to them and explore their fitness goals by improving their performance times in various events. An informal study of the competitors at the 1974 National Championships at Ft. Lauderdale revealed that one-third never swam in competition until Masters participation, one-third had high-school swimming experience, and one-third had collegiate experience or beyond (48, p. 38). There seem to be two groups of participants: (1) the superstars who are the strongest competitors, setting local and national records and recording the top ten times in the country in their events; and (2) the beginners and average swimmers, who set very few records but who strive for personal best times in their performances (10, p. 40).

A potential criticism of the Masters program is the mixing of all different types of swimmers into one competitive group. Inexperienced swimmers can be put at a tremendous and discouraging disadvantage when matched against more experienced competitors. Equality between competitors is a fundamental principle underlying all forms of competitive athletics. While there is always the satisfaction of improving your time in a certain event, an inexperienced swimmer will never compete successfully with a swimmer who has years of competitive background. Perhaps two divisions could be established to alleviate this problem: (1) a novice division for those who have never swum competitively before, and (2) a competitor division for those who swam competitively in high school, college, or beyond.

The problem is recognized by the organizers of Masters Swimming in their detailed age groupings for men and women, which are far more extensive than in the adult competitive running programs, but more attention must be given to the problem of equality between competitors within their age groupings to ensure a widespread base of support and participation (116, p. 8). Statistics show that the number of Masters swimmers is relatively small in comparison to the total number of swimmers in the United States today.

GOAL SETTING

Masters swimmers should set and continually reset some realistic personal goals for themselves in terms of training and/or competition. These long-term and short-term goals for health and performance should be based on level of fitness, stroke efficiency and potential, age and sex, time available, and physical or mental handicaps if any (79, p. 27). It should be emphasized that there is room in Masters swimming for many different people who can benefit from participation up to the limits of their own aspirations, interests and energy.

PHYSICAL ASPECTS

Effects of Aging Although peak performance in swimming is typically associated with young people, those Masters swimmers who become serious about competition can usually improve their individual performance times considerably. Several factors besides age affect performance, including "natural abilities, stroke efficiency, psychological attributes, and the amount of training time" (70, p. 28).

Ransom Arthur recognized the effectiveness of current training techniques when he said:

> Masters swimmers who have the time and physical strength to go to an all-out program can equal or exceed the times of their youth . . . no matter what they believe, they really do not have the muscular and cardio-vascular system they had when they were 20. It makes one realize how much faster they could have swum in 1952, say, had they trained by 1973 standards. (8, p. 41)

A person's physical capacities may begin to diminish with age and this may cause maximum performance efforts to level off, but not necessarily. If all other factors could somehow be held constant, and age were the only variable, then there would be a decline in performance of 1/2 – 1 percent a year (70, p. 28). Best performance is a complicated matter, however, and many factors may compensate for loss of physical abilities with aging and permit improved times in various events for the competitive-minded Masters swimmer who can maintain the necessary training program.

Medical Emergencies The most serious medical problem in Masters swimming is the possibility of a heart attack during training or competition. Meet sponsors must always be sure whom to call for help, that resuscitation equipment is available, that lifeguards and other personnel are trained in cardiopulmonary resuscitation (CPR) and other lifesaving skills, and that a complete emergency plan is thought out and rehearsed in advance. Paul Hutinger emphasized the importance of local access to a defibrillator, an electrical machine which is used (but only by medical doctors or trained technicians) to restart a heart that has stopped (80, p. 24).

Ransom Arthur suggested the following personal approach for each Masters swimmer (11, p. 49):

1. Read the article "How to Recognize—and Survive—A Heart Attack" by Richard Ames in *Reader's Digest*, November 1983, p. 110.
2. Carry major medical coverage and keep your card with you.
3. Do not dismiss chest pains as indigestion.
4. Make sure that there is a doctor in attendance when you compete.
5. Make sure that someone knows something about you if you are attending the meet alone.
6. Remember—it can happen to you.

Two other possible emergencies in Masters swimming are dehydration (9, p. 54) and hypoglycemia (7, p. 46). When training or competing under hot conditions, it is important to replace water and minerals that are lost during exercise. Although you may not realize it, remember that you do sweat during your swimming workouts. When competing over a period of several days, it is important to keep the blood sugar level up by eating regularly, even if lightly. It's best to be cautious and not push yourself too hard, especially under adverse circumstances. Use the scratch procedures to drop out of an event rather than risk more serious medical problems.

Water Temperature Water temperature can affect training and performance, and many Masters swimmers do not swim well in cold water. It has been found that 74–75° is too cold, 76–78° is not ideal, 80–82° is best for meets, and 82–84° is good for practice (12, p. 56). Meet sponsors should be sensitive to this problem and adjust and maintain pool temperatures accordingly.

OPEN WATER SWIMMING

There is a world of difference between swimming in a pool and swimming in open water (27, 38, 107, and 114). For one thing, official distances are often only estimates, and judging distances over the water can be very deceiving. Constantly changing conditions affect speed and performance over the same distance on different occasions. Tides, currents, undertows, rips, waves, and marine life also affect performance, so you should learn all you can about their influence. The cold water presents another risk to the swimmer, since water of a certain temperature conducts heat away from the body some 25 times faster than for the same air temperature on land.

Swimmers should follow certain guidelines when swimming in open water to reduce risk and perform better:

1. Never train or swim alone.

2. Know the direction and layout of the swimming course (parallel to shore, around buoys, straight across the lake, etc.).

3. Wear a bathing cap to help retain heat (30–50 percent of the body's heat is lost through the head) and to help observers and officials keep sight of you.

4. Practice in similar cold-water conditions, and know the symptoms and treatment of hypothermia (lowered body temperature).

5. Motion sickness can be overwhelming, and you'll need to test your reactions to various nonprescription medications for this problem.

6. Practice the procedures for releasing cramps in deep water. These can be very painful and devastating to a swimmer. Your hands, feet, and calves are especially susceptible to cramping problems. Warm up and stretch out before competing.

7. Vaseline should be used to prevent chafing, especially under your arm-pits and wherever your swimsuit might rub you, such as around your legs or under the shoulder straps. Men who don't shave on the day of the race may irritate the skin on their shoulder with the stubble of their beard. Vaseline on the beard can reduce this problem, but the real causes are probably mistiming of the breathing (breathing too late) and crossing over the midline of the body at the hand entry position.

8. If you are going to swim more than 2 hours, you should consider the use of high-calorie liquid supplements to feed on during your swim. This requires coordination with an assistant in an escort boat.

9. If an escort boat is to be used, you should practice to learn how to stay with the boat.

10. Practice looking forward periodically as you swim, because you have to be able to sight landmarks to maintain your direction.

11. Learn to tread water with your legs only so you'll be able to clear your goggles if they fill with water.

12. Practice hypoxic breathing patterns (breathe every second, third, fourth, or fifth stroke) at times in your workouts. You may have to skip a breath every now and then if you're trapped in a crowd of swimmers of if choppy waves are breaking over your head.

13. You should be able to breathe to either side (alternate side breathing) in crawl stroke. This will equalize stress on both sides, and permit you to breathe away from the waves if necessary.

14. While crawl stroke is best for most people, you may want to change strokes occasionally as a short break in a long swim.

15. A trained observer can count your strokes per minute, and this is the best standard of whether you're swimming at the right pace, swimming too slowly, or trying too hard. Normal references, such as lap times or speed per 100 yards, usually will not apply under these circumstances.

16. Most distance swimmers do not emphasize the kick in their stroke, using the kick more for body position and balance than for great propulsion. Do some specific kicking drills in your workouts, but don't overdo it.

17. Although 75–85 percent of your training should be long-distance swimming, remember that it's very easy to accommodate to this type of exercise by swimming very slowly. It's important to spend some of your training time doing fast interval work and sprints; this helps with conditioning, helps to keep your hand speed up, and gives you a reserve of power that may be needed in a race.

18. The start of the race is likely to be hectic, with swimmers jockeying for position and trying to find open water to swim in. Be prepared for this, or you'll be off to a bad start.

19. You must go through the official finishing point and check yourself out of the race when you're done. Race officials must have everyone accounted for, either dropped out or finished, in the interest of safety.

Be careful in your first open water competitions, and don't get carried away with fantasies of winning and setting records. As with any Masters event, experience will improve your performance if you strive to learn from your mistakes and successes. Just don't lose sight of two basic goals: complete the event and feel good about yourself afterward.

COACHING

Although there is some coaching available at the Masters level, not nearly enough attention has been given to the older age groups. For employed or volunteer coaches, Masters coaching can be fun, challenging, and rewarding in a developmental program with highly self-motivated adult swimmers. There is usually a wide range of abilities on Masters teams, and the coaches should strive constantly to individualize the training programs for everyone from beginning swimmers up to sophisticated performers. If full-time coaching is not available, sometimes adult clinics or camps, question-and-answer periods, and/or special help sessions can be arranged to assist Masters and fitness swimmers. For example, we have sponsored special clinics at Dickinson College for

Masters swimmers. These clinics focus on the needs and interests of the group; some of the topics have been:

- Alternate side breathing for crawl stroke
- Use of equipment in your training program
- Open turns and flip turns for crawl stroke
- Related competitive skills—starts, turns, finishes, and relays
- Stroke analysis—fly, back, breast, and crawl
- Hutinger's 24-minute swim test
- Guidelines for performance and competition
- Special help session (bring a swimming problem with you)
- Swimming the English Channel
- Individual Medley swimming
- Film analysis of strokes
- Race strategy for distance swimming
- Examples of distance swimming workouts
- Strength training programs
- Examples of short interval workouts

One area in which all serious Masters competitors should have coaching is following competition rules. Stroke and turn judges are usually employed during competition to make sure that performers are swimming their strokes in proper form. Judges tend to be lenient with inexperienced swimmers who seem to be trying their best but who do not have perfect form, provided they do not seek or gain any competitive advantage (14, p. 46). However, as Masters swimming continues to grow and competition becomes more keen, rule enforcement of this type will and should become more strict. Therefore, Masters competitors should have all aspects of their performance (start, stroke, turns, finish) checked by a rule-experienced coach or official so that they can work on problem areas and not get disqualified for violations of basic rules as they progress to higher levels of competition.

TRAINING INTENSITY

Paul Hutinger presented a program of great intensity which involved the use of high-quality, fast-speed repeat swims (72–74). This "Per Cent Effort Training" used low total yardage (5,000 yards per week) with training done every other day. The swimmer must use 80–90 percent effort for all basic repeats in his/her interval training program. Divide your best time for a distance by the desired percent to determine the repeat time. For example, if your best time for 50-yard crawl stroke is 27 seconds, then

$$\frac{27}{.80} = 33.8 \text{ seconds} \quad \text{and} \quad \frac{27}{.90} = 30 \text{ seconds}$$

This swimmer would need to do 50-yard crawl stroke repeats between 30 and 34 seconds to follow this training program. If your best time for 100-yard crawl stroke is 60 seconds, then

$$\frac{60}{.80} = 75 \text{ seconds or } 1{:}15 \text{ and}$$

$$\frac{60}{.90} = 66.6 \text{ seconds or } 1{:}06.6$$

This swimmer would need to do 100-yard crawl stroke repeats between 1:07 and 1:15 minutes to follow this training program.

Hutinger intended this program as an alternative for Masters swimmers to the programs involving long yardage and lower-intensity repeats, and he used it to maintain or improve his own competitive performance times. The program is extremely vigorous, with heart rates approaching maximum during each repeat swim. Rest periods must be of sufficient length to permit the swimmers to approach their best times over and over again as they repeat. Ransom Arthur cautioned:

> You need to monitor whether your body is up to these almost 100 percent efforts on a regular basis. Many individuals simply can't stand up to so much focused exertion. (16, p. 49)

Competitive swimmers should add these high-quality repeat workouts to their training programs but should not use them to the exclusion of other types of workouts. Check your own effort by dividing your best time by your repeat time. For example,

If 33 seconds is your best time for 50-yard crawl stroke, and you typically swim repeats at 45 seconds, then

$$\frac{33 \text{ seconds}}{45 \text{ seconds}} \quad = \quad .733 \quad = \quad 73\% \text{ effort}$$

If 1:13 is your best time for 100-yard crawl stroke, and you typically swim repeats at 1:35, then

$$\frac{1:13}{1:35} \quad = \quad \frac{73 \text{ seconds}}{95 \text{ seconds}} \quad = \quad .768 \quad = \quad 77\% \text{ effort}$$

Diane Lintner studied exercise intensity in swimming by determining the heart rate response to interval swimming at various percentages of the maximum speed (91). Subjects were initially tested for their fastest speed for 100 yards, and then were trained at speeds based on percentages of that speed. Training sessions consisted of 5×100-yard repeat swims at 60, 70 80, and 90 percent of maximum speed. Average heart rates were 127 beats per minute for 60 percent effort, 142 for 70 percent, 161 for 80 percent, and 170 for 90 percent.

Those swimmers who have health/fitness purposes can probably exercise mostly at 70–85 percent effort (occasionally with a higher percentage) and still achieve heart rates that will create beneficial training effects. Those swimmers who have competitive goals can probably work out mostly at 75–90 percent effort (occasionally more, occasionally less) in their pursuit of faster times. A good initial plan to create more variety and intensity in your workouts is to swim at least one quality repeat per set or at least one quality set per workout.

A LIFETIME WORKOUT PLAN

Ransom Arthur, recognizing that Masters swimmers need to develop a realistic workout plan if they are to stay with it for life, said that a lifetime plan should be:

of sufficient length, frequency and challenge as to maintain good cardio-pulmonary fitness, but short enough to fit comfortably into one's life pattern...should make one feel pleasantly fatigued but not exhausted... [should be] rigorous enough [to] make a creditable showing in meets [but]...insufficient to produce super times.

Influences of advancing age and greatly increased life responsibilities and demands make it quite impossible for me to sustain the hard workouts of previous years. . . . consequently I have had to rethink my entire personal swimming program. I wish to continue swimming for the rest of my life and I also wish to continue my participation in Masters meets indefinitely [but] adjustments have to be made in the workout to accommodate to a new reality. I also have to adjust to not achieving my best times of the past years but still making a respectable showing . . . this will be a dilemma for virtually all Masters swimmers and each one of you will have to [devise] your own individualized "perpetual workout" schedule which you can then do for years or even decades.

Remember the four objectives: a workout which will promote rather than tear down your health; one which you will enjoy; one which will keep you going indefinitely; and finally, one which will enable you to swim a race of which you don't feel ashamed. (*10*, p. 40)

REVIEW

Answer as many questions as you can by yourself, then refer to the chapter text or the Index to find the answers to the rest of the questions.

1. Age-group swimming competition for adults is called the _____.
2. Do you have any interest in a competitive program of training and meets? Why?
3. If you were to enter a Masters Swimming Meet, which events would you enter?
4. What are the differences between swimming in open water and swimming in a pool?
5. Physical performance is said to decline about_____percent a year, supposedly showing the influence of age on maximum speed.
6. Suggest some clinic topics for Masters swimmers that would be helpful to you.
7. CPR stands for_____. Are you, or any members of your family, trained in CPR?
8. What is meant by Per Cent Effort Training?
9. What is meant by a "perpetual workout schedule"?

CHAPTER TEN
Fitness Swimming Courses

This chapter presents seven courses in a self-paced or independent study format. In other words, you can complete these courses on your own, working by yourself and progressing at your own pace. This curriculum starts fitness swimmers at the very beginning and then takes them to increasingly difficult levels. Successful completion of all these courses would bring together most of the concepts and skills that have been emphasized throughout this book.

Some fitness swimmers will need to scale these courses up or down a little; you should personalize these standard programs as much as possible. These courses are only models to be used in the establishment of comprehensive programs for lifetime activity and enjoyment. All of the courses have been taught at the college level, and could easily be adapted for use in high schools and public agencies.

Despite initial enthusiasm, many people who start fitness programs eventually quit or continue in a haphazard manner. Apparently, this problem is widespread and cuts across all fitness activities. According to Patricia MacKeen: "Many people perhaps ought to try to stay in exercise programs and not assume that they can go out and do it on their own" (137). My theory is that many beginners quickly become bored with doing the same thing workout after workout, but don't know how to add variety to their workouts.

This problem is dealt with in Dickinson College's fitness swimming courses and club activities. I hope that you can participate in these seven courses many different times in many different ways and sequences, and that you can find many years of challenge in the completion of the club activities which are described in the next chapter. Continuous planned variety is one of the most important principles in constructing fitness programs that will last for a lifetime, and completion of these courses will help you construct such a program.

143

COURSE 1
FITNESS SWIMMING INTRODUCTION

Course 1 is a comprehensive introduction to swimming as a lifetime fitness activity. Most of the classes within this course are organized as follows:

1. Reading assignment to be done before you arrive at the pool.
2. Brief practice period in the pool on the topic of the class, or an appropriate review of previous classes.
3. Swimming workout period, including a special recommended procedure for you to try in addition to your own workout plan.

It is assumed that you will spend 25–35 minutes in the pool for each class. Always begin your workout with a short warm-up and finish with a short warm-down.

CLASS	CLASS CONTENT	COMPLETED
1	Review the Foreward and Preface, Chapter 1, and Chapter 2 as a general introduction to this course.	————
	Review the sections in Chapter 3 on bobbing and on flutter kicking and alternate side breathing.	————
	Practice bobbing in shallow water, and practice side breathing against the wall and with a kickboard. Work for 5–10 minutes total.	————
	Swim on your own as much as possible in the time you have left, including bobbing 8–10 times after each odd-numbered length and side breathing 8–10 times against the wall after each even-numbered length.	————
2	Review the remaining sections in Chapter 3 on various breathing patterns for crawl stroke.	————
	Practice the breathing patterns for crawl stroke: right side only, left side only, and alternate side patterns (1 to right and 1 to left, 2 to right and 2 to left, and 3 to right and 3 to left).	————
	Swim on your own, including the use of a different breathing pattern every 4th length.	————
	Note: Some fitness swimmers will need to repeat the Classes 1 and 2 periodically to learn all of these breathing patterns. They should not stop the course at this point, but should continue on with other classes, including brief practices on breathing patterns within the normal progression of their classes.	————

CLASS	CLASS CONTENT	COMPLETED
3	Review the sections in Chapter 7 on warm-up/warm-down procedures.	_____
	Practice as many of the stretching and flexibility exercises as you can in 5 minutes.	_____
	Swim on your own, including 4 lengths easy swimming warm-up and 2 lengths easy swimming warm-down.	_____
4	Review the sections in Chapter 6 on push-offs.	_____
	Practice the front push-off and the back push-off 4–5 times each.	_____
	Swim on your own, emphasizing good push-offs throughout your workout.	_____
5	Review the sections in Chapter 6 on the crawl stroke turn and the backstroke turn.	_____
	Practice the front and back push-offs 2 times each, and then practice the crawl stroke turn and the backstroke turn 4–5 times each.	_____
	Swim on your own, emphasizing good turns and push-offs throughout your workout.	_____
6	Review the section in Chapter 5 on the butterfly stroke.	_____
	Practice the butterfly stroke: use a pull buoy to practice the arm stroke, use a kickboard to practice the kick, swim the entire stroke, and work in the breathing pattern. Use ½ lengths for this stroke practice.	_____
	Swim on your own, including some butterfly every 8th length. Continue to work every class on increasing your distance with this stroke, up to 1–2 lengths.	_____
7	Review the sections in Chapter 6 on the remaining stroke turns.	_____
	Practice these stroke turns 2–3 times each.	_____
	Swim on your own, emphasizing good turns and push-offs throughout your workout.	_____
8	Review the section in Chapter 6 on individual medley turns.	_____
	Practice the IM turns 2–3 times each.	_____
	Swim on your own, including some work on IM swimming.	_____

CLASS	CLASS CONTENT	COMPLETED
	Try to build yourself up to a continuous 100 IM within the next few classes.	———
	Continue to emphasize good turns and push-offs throughout your workout.	———
9	Review Chapter 4 on equipment use, concentrating on equipment that is available at your pool.	
	Practice with each piece of equipment that you normally use for 1–2 minutes each.	———
	Swim on your own, including 5 minutes each with pieces of equipment that you normally don't use.	———
10	Review sections of the book that you've had difficulty with in classes 1–9.	———
	Practice skills that you've had difficulty with in classes 1–9.	———
	Swim on your own, including 6–10 one-length sprints at the end of your workout.	———
11	Review the section in Chapter 7 on continuous swimming and the section in Chapter 2 on intensity of exercise and the interpretation of heart rates.	———
	Check your heart rate carefully at the beginning, middle, and end of your workout.	———
	Swim on your own, but keep moving for the entire time period even if you have to walk or jog on the bottom of the pool periodically. Don't stop moving (except to check your heart rate).	———
	Review the section in Chapter 7 on sample workouts, and examine some of the lap swimming and timed workouts.	———
12	Review the section in Chapter 7 on interval training and the section in Chapter 2 on intensity of exercise and the interpretation of heart rates.	———
	Check your heart rate carefully at the beginning, middle, and end of your workout.	———
	Swim on your own, including 4–6 × 50 with 30–45 seconds rest between each.	———
	Review the section in Chapter 7 on sample workouts, and examine some of the interval workouts.	———

CLASS	CLASS CONTENT	COMPLETED
13	Review the section in Chapter 5 on the backstroke.	_____
	Practice the backstroke, emphasizing the pull, the kick, the breathing, and the coordination.	_____
	Swim on your own, including the following pyramid: 50/100/200/100/50.	_____
14	Review the section in Chapter 5 on the breaststroke.	_____
	Practice the breaststroke, emphasizing the pull, the kick, the breathing, and the coordination.	_____
	Swim on your own, including 4–6 ×100 with 1 minute rest between each.	_____
15	Review the section in Chapter 5 on the crawl stroke.	_____
	Practice the crawl stroke, emphasizing the pull, the kick, the breathing, and the coordination.	_____
	Swim on your own, including 3–4 × 50 descending times: each 50 faster.	_____
16	Review the section in Chapter 5 on the elementary backstroke.	_____
	Practice the elementary backstroke, emphasizing the pull, the kick, the breathing, and the coordination.	_____
	Swim on your own, including a *stroke only* workout—no crawl permitted in this workout.	_____
17	Review the section in Chapter 5 on the sidestroke.	_____
	Practice the sidestroke on both sides, emphasizing the pull, the kick, the breathing, and the coordination.	_____
	Swim on your own, including your own plan for a brief interval workout. Use 100s, 50s, and 25s, and be able to identify the four variables in your interval workout.	_____
18	Review sections of the book that you've had difficulty with in classes 11–17.	_____
	Practice skills that you've had difficulty with in classes 11–17.	_____
	100-yd. (4 lengths) Crawl Stroke Pulling Test—use a pull buoy, and maintain an alternate side breathing pattern for the entire distance.	_____

CLASS	CLASS CONTENT	COMPLETED
	300-yd. (12 lengths) Fin Kicking Test—use a kickboard and swim fins, and kick continuously for the entire distance using the following pattern: 50 fly K – 50 back K – 50 crawl K...	———
19	Review the section in Chapter 8 on aerobic swim tests.	———
	Cooper's 12-Minute Swim Test—Swim as far as possible in the time period, and compare your results to established norms.	———
	Individual Medley Swim Test—two 30-ft. widths each of the butterfly, back, breast, and crawl strokes continuously in that order, including the appropriate stroke and IM turns. Start in the water (no dive). Test should be done in a diving well using an area that is 30 ft. wide, but if you do not have a narrow area, use a normal lane and start 30 ft. out from the wall. Swim in and out continuously with each of the strokes doing the appropriate stroke turns. Change from stroke to stroke as best and as quickly as you can. Make sure that you are also proficient with the IM turns, since this procedure eliminates them from the test.	———
20	1-Mile Swim Test—swim continuously for 1 mile (70 lengths); you may change strokes as often as you wish but must keep moving. Use of equipment is not permitted.	———
	Skim the rest of Chapter 8 and all of Chapter 9	———
	Read Chapter 11.	———
	Advance to Course 2—Lap Swimming Workouts I.	———

COURSE 2
LAP SWIMMING WORKOUTS I

Course 2 involves the completion of a planned series of lap swimming workouts of increasing lengths. Your goals should be the continued refinement of your turns and push-offs; total familiarity with the pull buoy, kickboard, hand paddles, and swim fins; and the ability to change your workout patterns frequently. Use different swimming strokes; vary the amount of pulling, kicking, and swimming in each workout; use different pieces of equipment at times; rarely do the same workout twice. You may use the lap swimming workouts in Chapter 7, and/or you can make up your own lap swimming workouts as you become more comfortable with this format. Remember to start and finish your workouts with suitable warm-up/warm-down procedures.

CLASS	CLASS CONTENT	COMPLETED
1	Review the sections in Chapter 2 on the frequency, intensity, and duration of exercise, and on variety in your training program; the sections in Chapter 7 on warm-up/warm-down procedures, sample workouts, and lap swimming workouts; and Chapters 4 and 6.	———
2	Workout—20 lengths	———
3	Workout—20 lengths	———
4	Workout—26 lengths	———
5	Workout—26 lengths	———
6	Workout—26 lengths	———
7	Workout—32 lengths	———
8	Workout—32 lengths	———
9	Workout—32 lengths	———
10	Use this book to review problem areas. Practice problem skills in the pool. Brief workout with your choice of the total number of lengths.	——— ——— ———
11	Workout—38 lengths	———
12	Workout—38 lengths	———
13	Workout—44 lengths	———
14	Workout—44 lengths	———
15	Workout—44 lengths	———
16	Workout—50 lengths	———
17	Workout—50 lengths	———
18	Workout—50 lengths	———
19	80-Lengths Test—prepare your own workout plan for this distance in a lap swimming format. Use as much variety as possible in your sets and subsets. Question: 80 lengths = ____ yards?	——— ———

CLASS	CLASS CONTENT	COMPLETED
20	Cooper's 12-Minute Swim Test—swim as far as possible in the time period, and compare your results to established norms. Also compare your results to your first attempt at this test in Course 1. Some fitness swimmers find it very motivating to take this test once or twice a year, charting their results and noting their fitness categories.	————
	Advance to Course 3—Timed Workouts I.	———— ————

Note to beginning Fitness Swimmers: You can scale the workout distances down to meet your needs. For example, one student began this course with 10 lengths and increased by 4 lengths each week, completing the following schedule:

1st week—2 workouts at 10 lengths each
2nd week—3 workouts at 14 lengths each
3rd week—3 workouts at 18 lengths each
4th week—2 workouts at 22 lengths each
5th week—3 workouts at 26 lengths each
6th week—3 workouts at 30 lengths each
7th week—40 lengths for testing distance

You must also use considerable judgment in taking the 12-minute test. This student took the test, but the instructor did not compare her distance to the established norms. Objectively, she would not have been placed in a very high fitness category. Subjectively, however, she left the course somewhat amazed that she could swim for 12 minutes and pleased with her progressive accomplishments during the 7 weeks. Feeling good about yourself is certainly an important aspect of the fitness swimming experience. You must be cautious and use good sense when interpreting general standards and categories that do not take your starting point into account.

COURSE 3
TIMED WORKOUTS I

Course 3 involves the completion of a planned series of timed workouts, which increase by minutes rather than lengths. By this point in the sequence of courses, you should be very familiar with such basic exercise principles as frequency, intensity, duration, warm-up/warm-down, and variety. Your turns and push-offs should be well executed in the water, and you should be using equipment at times during your workout. Your goals for this course should be total mastery of all the breathing patterns for crawl stroke and the continued development of the various swimming strokes. Your ability to change workout patterns frequently should continue to expand. You may write your own timed workouts or use the examples in Chapter 7.

CLASS	CLASS CONTENT	COMPLETED
1	Review the sections in Chapter 3 on alternate side breathing patterns for crawl stroke, Chapter 5, and the sections in Chapter 7 on sample workouts and timed workouts.	_____
2	Workout—10 minutes	_____
3	Workout—10 minutes	_____
4	Workout—15 minutes	_____
5	Workout—15 minutes	_____
6	Workout—15 minutes	_____
7	Workout—20 minutes	_____
8	Workout—20 minutes	_____
9	Workout—20 minutes	_____
10	Use this book to review problem areas. Practice problem skills in the pool. Brief workout with your choice of the total number of minutes.	_____ _____ _____
11	Workout—25 minutes	_____
12	Workout—25 minutes	_____
13	Workout—25 minutes	_____
14	Workout—30 minutes	_____
15	Workout—30 minutes	_____
16	Workout—30 minutes	_____
17	Workout—35 minutes	_____
18	Workout—35 minutes	_____
19	Workout—35 minutes	_____
20	50-minute Test—prepare your own workout plan for 50 minutes in a timed workout format. Use as much variety as possible in your sets and subsets. Advance to Course 4—Interval Workouts I.	_____ _____

COURSE 4
INTERVAL WORKOUTS I

Course 4 involves the completion of a planned series of interval workouts, with all distances given in yards. Your principal goal is to become totally familiar with interval training procedures and variables. You may use the interval workouts in Chapter 7, or make up your own interval workouts as you become more comfortable with this format. Remember to use appropriate warm-up/warm-down procedures for each workout.

CLASS	CLASS CONTENT	COMPLETED
1	Review the following sections in Chapter 7: converting lengths to yards and vice-versa, interval training (repeat swimming), and sample workouts and interval workouts.	_____
2	Workout—500 yards	_____
3	Workout—500 yards	_____
4	Workout—600 yards	_____
5	Workout—600 yards	_____
6	Workout—700 yards	_____
7	Workout—700 yards	_____
8	Workout—800 yards	_____
9	Workout—800 yards	_____
10	Use this book to review problem areas. Review problem skills in the pool. Brief interval workout with your choice of the total number of yards.	_____ _____ _____
11	Workout—900 yards	_____
12	Workout—900 yards	_____
13	Workout—1,000 yards	_____
14	Workout—1,000 yards	_____
15	Workout—1,100 yards	_____
16	Workout—1,100 yards	_____
17	Workout—1,200 yards	_____
18	Workout—1,200 yards	_____
19	Workout—1,000 yards	_____
20	1-Mile Test—prepare your own interval workout for 1,750 yards. Include as much variety as possible in your sets and subsets. Advance to Course 5—Lap Swimming Workouts II.	_____ _____

COURSE 5
LAP SWIMMING WORKOUTS II

Course 5 involves the completion of a planned series of lap swimming workouts which vary randomly in length from 40 to 70 lengths.

CLASS	CLASS CONTENT	COMPLETED
1	Use this book to review problem areas.	_____
	Practice problem skills in the pool.	_____
	Brief workout with your choice of the total number of lengths.	_____
2	Workout—40 lengths	_____
3	Workout—52 lengths	_____
4	Workout—64 lengths	_____
5	Workout—42 lengths	_____
6	Workout—54 lengths	_____
7	Workout—66 lengths	_____
8	Workout—44 lengths	_____
9	Workout—56 lengths	_____
10	Use this book to review problem areas.	_____
	Practice problem skills in the pool.	_____
	Brief workout with your choice of the total number of lengths	_____
11	Workout—68 lengths	_____
12	Workout—46 lengths	_____
13	Workout—50 lengths	_____
14	Workout—60 lengths	_____
15	Workout—48 lengths	_____
16	Workout—58 lengths	_____
17	Workout—70 lengths	_____
18	Workout—62 lengths	_____
19	Workout—40 lengths	_____
20	100-Lengths Swim Test—swim continuously for 100 lengths, using a counting device to keep track of your lengths. You may change strokes as often as you wish, but keep moving. Use of equipment is not permitted.	_____
	Question: 100 lengths = ____yards?	
	Advance to Course 6—Timed Workouts II.	_____

COURSE 6
TIMED WORKOUTS II

Course 6 involves the completion of a planned series of timed workouts which vary randomly from 20 to 50 minutes.

CLASS	CLASS CONTENT	COMPLETED
1	Workout—20 minutes	_____
2	Workout—32 minutes	_____
3	Workout—44 minutes	_____
4	Workout—22 minutes	_____
5	Workout—34 minutes	_____
6	Workout—46 minutes	_____
7	Use this book to review problem areas.	_____
	Practice problem skills in the pool.	_____
	Brief workout with your choice of the total number of minutes.	_____
8	Workout—24 minutes	_____
9	Workout—36 minutes	_____
10	Workout—48 minutes	_____
11	Workout—26 minutes	_____
12	Workout—38 minutes	_____
13	Workout—42 minutes	_____
14	Use this book to review problem areas.	_____
	Practice problem skills in the pool.	_____
	Brief workout with your choice of the total number of minutes.	_____
15	Workout—28 minutes	_____
16	Workout—30 minutes	_____
17	Workout—40 minutes	_____
18	Workout—50 minutes	_____
19	Workout—20 minutes	_____
20	1-hour Swim Test—swim continuously for 60 minutes, using a counting device to keep track of your distance. You may change strokes as often as you wish, but keep moving. Use of equipment is not permitted.	_____
	Advance to Course 7—Interval Workouts II.	_____

COURSE 7
INTERVAL WORKOUTS II

Course 7 involves the completion of a planned series of interval workouts which vary randomly in length from 1,000 to 1,750 yards.

CLASS	CLASS CONTENT	COMPLETED
1	Use this book to review problem areas.	_____
	Practice problem skills in the pool.	_____
	Brief workout with your choice of the total number of yards.	_____
2	Workout—1,000 yards	_____
3	Workout—1,300 yards	_____
4	Workout—1,600 yards	_____
5	Workout—1,050 yards	_____
6	Workout—1,350 yards	_____
7	Workout—1,650 yards	_____
8	Workout—1,100 yards	_____
9	Workout—1,400 yards	_____
10	Use this book to review problem areas.	_____
	Practice problem skills in the pool.	_____
	Brief interval workout with your choice of the total number of yards.	_____
11	Workout—1,700 yards	_____
12	Workout—1,150 yards	_____
13	Workout—1,250 yards	_____
14	Workout—1,500 yards	_____
15	Workout—1,200 yards	_____
16	Workout—1,450 yards	_____
17	Workout—1,750 yards	_____
18	Workout—1,550 yards	_____
19	Workout—1,000 yards	_____
20	2,500 Yard Interval Workout Test—complete the following workout: 800 P crawl—warm-up 800 5 × 100 S crawl on_____ 500 easy 100 K 100 10 × 50 S crawl on_____ 500 easy 100 P 100 8 × 25 sprint 200 300 fin K—warm-down 300 2,500 yds.	_____

CHAPTER ELEVEN
Fitness Swimming Club

Some people find it helpful to have the support of a group to keep themselves active over a long time period, and a fitness swimming club provides a loose network for this support. It is hoped that readers can modify the activities of the Dickinson College Fitness Swimming Club described in this chapter for use in their own settings.

MEMBERSHIP

There are two categories of membership in our Fitness Swimming Club: inducted members and noninducted members. Official induction into the Club follows the completion of 100 miles of swimming workouts. These one-time-only "membership dues" (i.e., 100 miles) are a realistic one-year project for most regular fitness swimmers. Swimmers declare their intention to become an inducted member, and then keep track of their swimming lengths or yards in a daily log (Figure 11-1). After completing 100 miles, each swimmer is awarded a certificate (Figure 11-2) to verify his/her inducted status, and his/her name is inscribed on a permanent plaque of inducted members which is displayed in the lobby of the pool. Noninducted members may participate in the Club activities but are not recognized with the certificate and plaque until they have completed their 100 miles.

INSTRUCTIONAL PROGRAMS

The formal instructional program usually includes a course that is taught over the Christmas break. For example, the Club has sponsored lifesaving and snorkel diving courses during that time. Another example was "Swim the English Channel," a course that included viewing two films of world-record English Channel swim attempts and a slide/sound presentation on cold water survival, and taking a 2-minute cold shower (well, at least a few people did this part). Swimmers were asked to read current and historical accounts of Channel crossings, as well as material about hypothermia and motivation for this kind of athletic performance. Each class member swam 21 miles during the course, broken up into short personal workouts. Distances were recorded and displayed on a large wall chart, and certificates and patches were issued upon completion of the course.

Another feature of the formal instructional program is a series of beginning swimming classes for adults. These classes start with a discussion of what the beginning swimmer actually hopes to accomplish during the course. The course content includes strokes (crawl, back, breast, elementary back), breathing exercises, and use of equipment, but it is always personalized to the needs, weaknesses, and interests of the swimmer. Usually, the instructor and student meet twice each week, with the understanding that the student will swim once more on his/her own

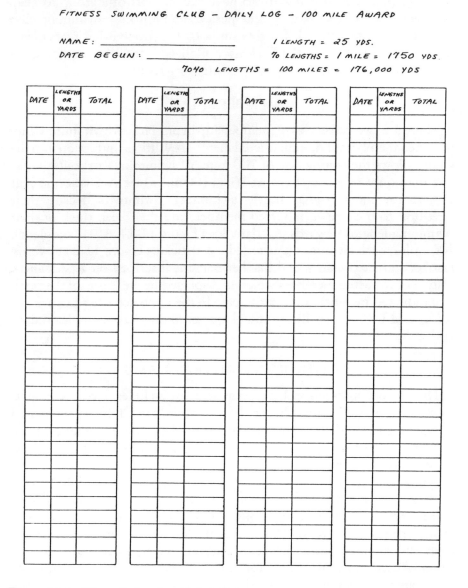

Figure 11-1. Fitness Swimming Club daily log.

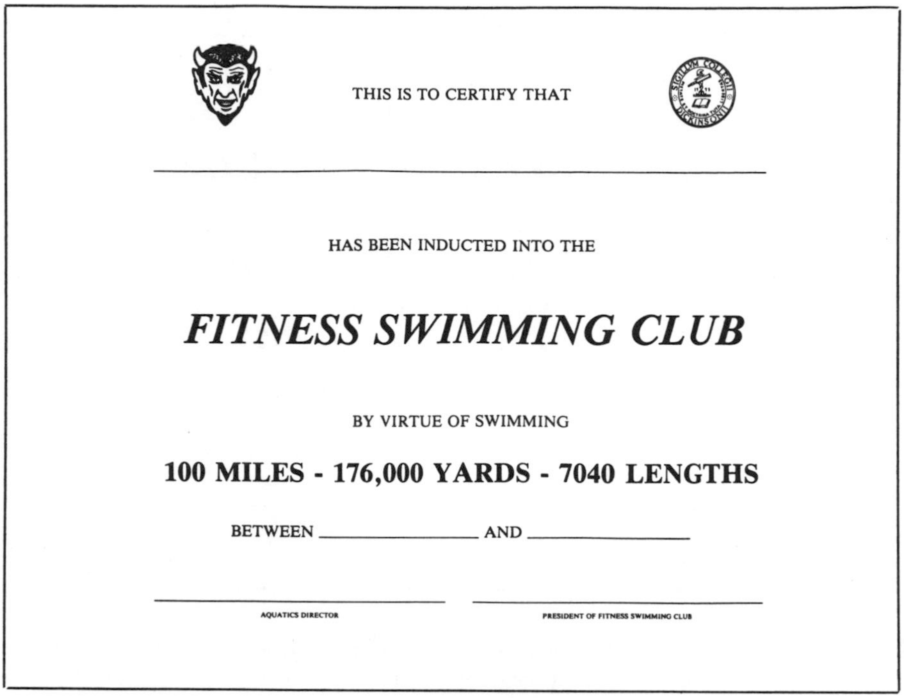

THIS IS TO CERTIFY THAT

_____

HAS BEEN INDUCTED INTO THE

FITNESS SWIMMING CLUB

BY VIRTUE OF SWIMMING

100 MILES - 176,000 YARDS - 7040 LENGTHS

BETWEEN _____ AND _____

_____   _____
AQUATICS DIRECTOR   PRESIDENT OF FITNESS SWIMMING CLUB

Figure 11-2. Fitness Swimming Club membership certificate.

during that week. In this one-on-one type of instruction, each class is 25–30 minutes long and the whole course runs for 6 weeks.

Our informal instructional program usually goes on during the noon hour, when some teaching and coaching is provided for those who want special help. This program is very flexible in order to be responsive to requests from individuals and small groups. We hope that our regular clientele feel that they can ask for help and receive it whenever they swim.

SPECIAL AWARDS

The Fitness Swimming Club has a variety of special awards to challenge swimmers. Swimmers who complete these challenges are awarded certificates such as the one shown in Figure 11-3.

SUPER SWIMS

Super Swims are a series of long, continuous swims without any equipment. They challenge the fitness swimmers by requiring them to swim longer and further than they normally do in their daily workouts. Club members are encouraged to finish each of the school semesters (4-month periods) by selecting and completing one of the following Super Swims (distance in yards): 2,500; 3,000; 3,500; 4,000; 4,500; 5,000;

159

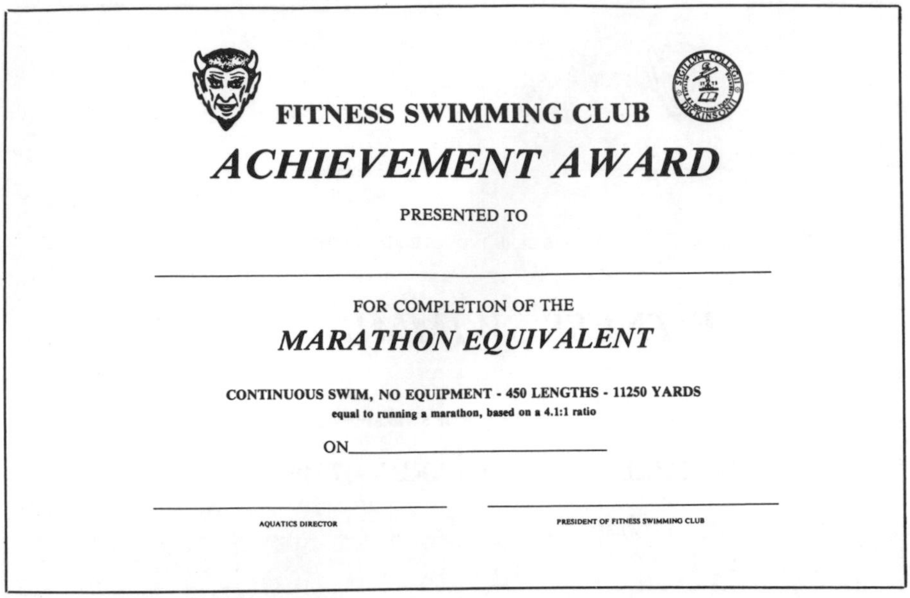
FITNESS SWIMMING CLUB

ACHIEVEMENT AWARD

PRESENTED TO

FOR COMPLETION OF THE

MARATHON EQUIVALENT

CONTINUOUS SWIM, NO EQUIPMENT - 450 LENGTHS - 11250 YARDS

equal to running a marathon, based on a 4.1:1 ratio

ON

AQUATICS DIRECTOR

PRESIDENT OF FITNESS SWIMMING CLUB

Figure 11-3. Marathon Equivalent certificate. (Appropriate certificates are awarded for the other special events described in the text.)

5,500; 6,000; 7,000; or 7,500. You must keep moving during the Super Swims, and you may mix up your strokes in any order that you choose. Small counting devices are provided to keep track of the lengths as accurately as possible. As an added challenge, some fitness swimmers elect to do only one stroke for the entire distance instead of a long mixer.

Super Workout Day

The objective of Super Workout Day is to swim 10,000 yards (400 lengths) in one day. You may rest whenever you want, but you are not permitted to use any equipment. You may mix up the strokes in any manner that you choose, or swim only crawl stroke the whole way. Some possible ways of completing this are

- 100 × 100 yd. repeat swims
- 5 × 2,000 S
- 4,000 S – 3,000 S – 2,000 S – 1,000 S
- 10,000 continuous swim
- 10 × 1,000 S on 45 minutes
- 20 × 500 S on 30 minutes

Although somewhat commonplace in competitive swimming now, this distance represents a substantial challenge to the average fitness swimmer.

1-MILE INDIVIDUAL MEDLEY

The 1-Mile Individual Medley is a continuous 1,800-yard swim consisting of 18 lengths butterfly, 18 lengths back, 18 lengths breast, and 18 lengths crawl in that order. This is the "ultimate IM," and the secret is to swim the butterfly stroke *very slowly* in the initial 450-yard segment.

MARATHON EQUIVALENT

The Marathon Equivalent is a long, continuous swim with no equipment. Using the 4.1:1 ratio that compares running to swimming, we found that swimming 450 lengths (11,250 yards) in a 25-yard pool is equivalent to the running marathon distance (26 miles, 385 yards). As in the Super Swims, keep moving, mix up your strokes or stay with the same stroke, and use a counting device to keep track of the distance.

200-MILES-IN-1 YEAR AWARD

An award is given to swimmers who complete 200 miles in 1 year. This award is highly challenging because the total distance (352,000 yards) requires the swimmer to maintain an average distance of approximately 1000 yards per day throughout the entire year. A daily log is used to record the actual distances completed in each workout, and this award represents a substantial commitment in terms of personal time and consistent effort. The award originated primarily for our Masters swimmers, but is certainly realistic for our fitness swimmers as well. For example, a fitness swimmer could achieve the distance by swimming 1 mile four times a week for 50 weeks.

WORKOUT OF THE WEEK

Every Monday, a new fitness swimming workout of the week is posted. Different formats are used (lap swimming, timed, interval), and different distances are called for each week. This procedure adds variety and challenge to the workouts of our serious fitness swimmers. It forces them to move away from just swimming laps to following a preplanned and structured workout. They learn to interpret the different symbols that are commonly used in writing workouts. They become more familiar with the use of the pace clock, and more sensitive to the elements of time/speed/intensity in their training program. To get them even more involved, sometimes the club members are asked to prepare workout-of-the-week plans.

Some examples of the weekly workouts are presented here.

2 lengths—S crawl
4 lengths—S breast
6 lengths—S back
8 lengths—S crawl
───
20 lengths total

---

10 lengths—P crawl with hand paddles
10 lengths—S backstroke
10 lengths—P crawl R–L
10 lengths—S breaststroke
10 lengths—S crawl with flip turns
───
50 lengths total

---

6 min. - crawl
3 min. - fly K with fins, on your back
6 min. - crawl
3 min. - crawl K with fins, on your side
2 min. - easy
───
20 minutes total

---

7 min. - mixer
3 min. - fly K, no fins
8 min. - mixer
2 min. - back K, no fins
9 min. - mixer
1 min. - crawl K, no fins
1 min. - easy
───
31 minutes total

---

200 mixer warm-up	200
2 × 100—1 back, 1 elementary back	200
4 × 50 crawl	200
8 × 25—2 back, 2 breast, 2 crawl, 2 easy	200
	───
	800 yards

---

5 × 200 S crawl alternated with	1,000
5 × 100—1 S back	500
1 S breast	───
1 R–L–R–L	1,500 yards
1 S breast	
1 S back	

OTHER ACTIVITIES

Someone from our Club has tried (or will try) all of the following events or activities: 1-hour swim (how far can you swim in 1 hour); 10,000-meter swim (10 kilometers or 6.2 miles, a standard distance for running races); 10 minute kicking (how far can you kick in 10 minutes); the 1,750 yard Individual Medley (the "Iron Person" award for 50 fly – 50 back – 50 breast – 50 crawl – 50 side . . .); open water swims (in rivers, lakes, or oceans); overseas trips (for competition, training, and socializing); biathlons (continuous running/swimming events); triathlons (continuous swim/bike/run events); and the Super Swim (almost 2 miles— 132 lengths of a 25 yard pool, 3,300 yards—swimming against time standards based on age, sex, and ability levels). Club members are constantly on the search for new challenges and greater variety; *Swim Swim Magazine (131)* has become a valuable resource for them.

POOL SCHEDULE AND RULES

Our free swim schedule includes a substantial number of hours during which people can use the pool for fitness swimming. We are open 70–80 hours a week during the school year, 60–65 hours a week during summer school, and 20–25 hours a week during school vacations. We are usually able to keep several lanes open for free swim even during our scheduled classes, because the pool is large enough and the class sizes are manageable. We like to think of the pool as having hours that are very similar to the college library, with our regular clientele using the pool at their convenience from early in the morning until late in the evening. In fact, the Club begins each school year with an "early bird" workout on the first day of classes at 6:30 A.M. Most of the group aims toward a 1-mile workout at this time. A group breakfast follows the workout, which has been an especially nice way to bring the Club together at the start of each new school year.

The total availability of the pool is very conducive to fitness swimming, and the pool rules reinforce this supportive environment:

1. Lap swimming is the primary feature of our free swim hours. Do not interfere in any way with those who are swimming laps.

2. The swimming lanes are primarily for those who are swimming laps. The open area (or lanes 1 and 8 when all the lane lines are in) is primarily for those who are not swimming laps. Please be prepared to adjust to different levels of use (more people or less people using the pool).

3. You may not always be able to have your own lane every time you swim. Two swimmers can share a lane if they each stay on their own side of the lane. Three or more swimmers can circle within the lane, going down one side and coming back along the other side of the lane, spaced out 5–8 yards apart.

163

4. The use of swim goggles is highly recommended to our regular clientele.

5. If you use any of the swimming equipment, please put it back into the storage areas. Theft or intentional damage to this equipment will result in your expulsion from the facility.

6. Do not sit or hang on the surface lane lines. Go under them to switch lanes—do not lift them up.

7. Do not cut across the lanes. Follow the natural traffic patterns created by the surface and bottom lane lines.

8. Please enter the swimming pool only at the 4-ft. end. Do not dive in and do not use the starting blocks. Never risk serious neck and spinal injuries by diving head-first into shallow water.

9. Please stay off the bulkhead or wall which separates the swimming and diving pools.

10. No running—no pushing—no dunking—no wrestling—no horseplay—no towel snapping—no screaming.

11. No playing catch, water polo, water basketball, water volleyball, etc., except as specially scheduled.

12. Do not interfere in any way with scheduled classes or instructional programs.

13. Please refrain from all forms of questionable behavior.

14. Please check with the lifeguard or Aquatics Director if you have any questions, problems, or suggestions, or if there are any rules that you do not understand.

AN INVITATION

Readers of this book are invited to participate in some of the activities of the Dickinson College Fitness Swimming Club. You can officially join the Club as an affiliate member by swimming a total of 100 miles and submitting a documented log which records your distances to Dr. Joseph E. McEvoy, Fitness Swimming Club, Dickinson College, Carlisle PA 17013. As you complete other challenges (11 Super Swims, Super Workout Day, 1,800-yard Individual Medley, Marathon Equivalent, 200 Miles a Year), submit a letter which records the achievement, the date, and the distance. You will receive by mail a certificate which verifies your performance. If you are traveling in this area, plan to stop in and try the current Workout of the Week (please call in advance of your arrival to arrange the details).

A Fitness Swimming Hot Line (717-245-1523) has been established to provide help with your exercise program. Please limit your calls to between 12:00 noon and 1:00 P.M. (Eastern Standard Time), on Mondays only. If I am not available during this time, leave your name and number and I will return your call as soon as possible. This will give you a chance to talk about special needs and problems, and to ask any questions that you might have.

REFERENCES AND
FURTHER READINGS

1. Aguilar, Nona, "Swimming—How to Stay Super Fit In Only One Hour a Week," *Family Circle*, July 17, 1979, p. 96.

2. American Red Cross, *Swim and Stay Fit*, ARC 2149, Washington, D.C.: May 1976.

3. "America's Fitness Binge," *U.S. News & World Report*, May 3, 1982, pp. 58–61.

4. Ames, Richard, "How to Recognize—And Survive—A Heart Attack," *Reader's Digest*, November 1973, p. 110.

5. Arthur, Ransom J., "Masters Corner," *Swimming World*, March 1971, p. 36.

6. ———, "Masters Corner," *Swimming World*, November 1971, p. 23.

7. ———, "Masters Corner," *Swimming World*, July 1972, p. 46.

8. ———, "Masters Corner," *Swimming World*, July 1973, p. 41.

9. ———, "Masters Corner," *Swimming World*, October 1973, p. 54.

10. ———, "Masters Corner," *Swimming World*, November 1973, p. 40.

11. ———, "Masters Corner," *Swimming World*, January 1974, p. 49.

12. ———, "Masters Corner," *Swimming World*, August 1974, p. 56.

13. ———, "Masters Corner," *Swimming World*, October 1974, p. 54.

14. ———, "Masters Corner," *Swimming World*, June 1975, p. 46.

15. ———, "Masters Corner," *Swimming World*, June 1976, p. 47.

16. ———, "Masters Corner," *Swimming World*, February 1977, p. 49.

17. ———, "Masters Corner," *Swimming World*, March 1980, p. 87.

18. ———, personal communication, May 12, 1978.

19. ———, personal communication, August 15, 1978.

20. ———, phone communication, May 10, 1978.

21. Ayres, Ed, "The Myth of Indestructibility," *Running Times*, January 1979, pp. 15 – 18.

22. *Back Stroke—Women*, Aquaforums Films, P.O. Box 8, Champlain, NY 12919.

23. Barnard, R.J., et al., "Cardiovascular Response to Sudden Strenuous Exercise," *Journal of Applied Physiology* 34: 833 – 837, 1973.

24. Barnard, R.J., "Warm Up is Important for the Heart," *Sports Medicine Bulletin*, January 1975, p. 6.

25. Biosig, Inc., "Insta-Pulse—Heart Rate Monitor" (1979), P.O. Box 651, NDG, Montreal, Quebec, H4A 3R1, Canada.

26. *Breast Stroke—Women*, Aquaforums Films, P.O. Box 8, Champlain, NY 12919.

27. Brems, Marianne, "Racing—Open Water Swimming," *Swim Swim Magazine*, Summer 1982, p. 13.

28. ———, *Swim for Fitness*, San Francisco: Chronicle Books, 1979.

29. Bruning, Nancy P., *Swimming for Fitness*, New York: Dell Purse Books, 1979.

30. *Butterfly—Men*, Aquaforums Films, P.O. Box 8, Champlain, N.Y. 12919.

31. Castronis, Mike, "Jog in the Pool—No Pain!" *Journal of Physical Education* 74 (1):8, 1976.

32. Chusid, Joseph G., *Correlative Neuroanatomy and Functional Neurology*, 15th ed., Los Altos, CA: Lange Medical Publications, 1973.

33. Citrin, Stuart, "The Swimmer's Log—Training Too Hard?" *Aquatic World*, July 1976, p. 5.

34. Cooper, Kenneth H., *Aerobics*, New York: Bantam Books, 1968.

35. ———, *The Aerobics Program for Total Well-Being*, New York: M. Evans & Co., Inc., 1982.

36. ———, *The Aerobics Way*, New York: Bantam Books, Inc., 1977.

37. ———, *The New Aerobics*, New York: Bantam Books, Inc., 1970.

38. Counsilman, James E., "Advice to Rough Water Swimmers," *Rough Water Swimming Handbook*, Summer 1981, pp. 4 – 8.

39. ———, *Guidelines for Use of the Counsilman Drag Suit*, Rochester N.Y.: Training Equipment Corporation, 1979.

40. ———, "Hand Speed and Acceleration," *Swimming Technique*, May – July 1981, pp. 22 – 26.

41. ———, personal communication, July 1982.

42. ———, "Physiological Basis for a Two Week Cyclical Training Program" (mimeo). †

43. ———, "The Role of Sculling Movements in the Arm Pull, Part I," *Swimming World*, December 1969, p. 6.

44. ———, *The Science of Swimming*, Englewood Cliffs, N.J.: Prentice Hall, Inc., 1968.

45. Craig, Albert B. Jr., and Maria Dvorak, "Comparison of Exercise in Air and in Water of Different Temperatures," *Medicine and Science in Sports*, 1 (3): 124 – 130, 1969.

46. Cree, Elayne, "Swimmers Who Defy Time," *Sunday, The Hartford Courant Magazine*, January 21, 1979, pp. 3 – 7.

47. Cureton, Thomas K., "Factors Governing Success in Competitive Swimming—A Brief Review of Related Studies," *Swim-Master*, October 1973, pp. 1 – 2.

48. Dawson, Buck, "Masters Nationals—Highlights of Busiest Hall of Fame Spring," *Swimming World*, July 1974, p. 38.

49. de Barbadillo, John, "The YMCA Masters Swimming Program," mimeographed, December 1980. (Available from 1765 Wallace Street, York, PA 17402.)

50. Department of Continuing Education, Harvard Medical School, "Periodic Health Exams in Perspective," *Harvard Medical School Letter*, (9): 1-4, July 1980.

51. Detry, Jean-Marie R., et al., "Diagnostic Value of History and Maximal Exercise Electrocardiography in Men and Women Suspected of Coronary Heart Disease," *Circulation*, 56 (5): 756 – 761, 1977.

52. Evans, Blanche W., Kirk J. Cureton, and Jamie W. Purvis, "Metabolic and Circulatory Responses to Walking and Jogging in Water," *Research Quarterly*, 49 (4): 442 – 449, 1978.

53. "Exercise Could Be Hazardous To Your Health," *Changing Times*, April 1980, pp. 26 – 29.

54. "Exercise is Treatment for Anxiety," *Atlanta Journal*, p. 2-B. †

55. "FFM Swim Belt," (in 1981 Catalog) Pull-Buoy, Inc., 2511 Leach Rd., Auburn Heights, Michigan 48057.

56. Fixx, James F., "I Hurt More but I Feel Better—The Boston Marathon No One Tells You About," *Sky*, March 1977, pp. 30 – 32.

57. Furlong, William Barry, "The Fun in Fun," *Psychology Today*, June 1976, pp. 35 – 38, 80.

58. Getchell, Bud, *Physical Fitness—A Way of Life*, New York: John Wiley & Sons, Inc., 1976.

59. Gilmore, C.P., "Does Exercise Really Prolong Life?" *Reader's Digest*, July 1977, pp. 140 – 143.

60. Glasser, William, *Positive Addiction*, New York: Harper & Row, Publishers, 1976.

61. Green, Michelle,"The Joys and Hazards of Exercise," *Atlanta Journal and Constitution Magazine*, June 26, 1977, p. 12.

62. Hall, Gary, "Hand Paddles May Cause Shoulder Pain," *Swimming World*, September 1980, pp. 9 – 11.

63. Harper, Suzanne, "Exercise Intellectualized," *Nutshell*, pp. 89 – 91. †

64. Harris, Dorothy V., *Involvement in Sport: A Somatopsychic Rationale for Physical Activity*, Philadelphia: Lea & Febiger, 1973.

65. "Heart Report Calls Stress Test Useless," *Atlanta Journal*, August 2, 1979, pp. 1A, 16A.

66. Higdon, Hal, "Go Jump in the Lake," *The Runner*, April 1982, pp. 62 – 63.

67. Holmer, Ingvar, Anders Lundin, and Bengt O. Eriksson, "Maximum Oxygen Uptake during Swimming and Running by Elite Swimmers," *Journal of Applied Physiology*, 36 (6): 711 – 714, 1974.

68. Holt, Laurence E., *Scientific Stretching for Sport (3-S)*. (Available from author, Dalhousie University, Halifax, Nova Scotia.)

69. Huey, Pamela J., "A Legacy of Fitness and Good Health," *The Evening Sentinel* (Carlisle, Pa.), July 19, 1980, p. C22.

70. Hutinger, Paul, "Advice for the Swimmer's Body—Effects on Aging Performance," *Aquatic World*, January 1976, p. 28.

71. ———, "Advice for the Swimmer's Body—Exercising Regularly," *Aquatic World*, September 1976, p. 27.

72. ———, "Advice for the Swimmer's Body—Improve Performance," *Aquatic World*, March 1976, p. 30.

73. ———, "Advice for the Swimmer's Body—Little Training Time," *Aquatic World*, July 1976, p. 28.

74. ———, "Advice for the Swimmer's Body—Per Cent Effort Training," *Aquatic World*, January 1976, p. 28.

75. ———, "Advice for the Swimmer's Body—Short Races," *Aquatic World*, September 1975, p. 28.

76. ———, "Advice for the Swimmer's Body—Warm Up," *Aquatic World*, November 1975, p. 26.

77. ———, "Aerobic Capacities," *Aquatic World*, January 1976, p. 20.

78. ———, "The 'Fountain' of Youth," *Aquatic World*, November 1974, p. 18.

79. ———, "Hints for Masters," *Aquatic World*, July 1975, p. 27.

80. ———, "Pumping You through Your Laps," *Aquatic World*, January 1975, p. 22.

81. ———, "Warm-ups," *Aquatic World*, May 1975, p. 6.

82. Israel, Marvin, personal communication, May 19, 1980.

83. Johnson, Ruth, "Aerobic Swimming," *Aquatic World*, November 1976, p. 12.

84. Johnson, William Oscar, "Marching to Euphoria," *Sports Illustrated*, July 14, 1980, pp. 72–82.

85. Katz, Jane with Nancy Bruning, *Swimming for Total Fitness*, Garden City, N.Y.: Dolphin Books (Doubleday & Company, Inc.), 1981.

86. "Keeping Fit: America Tries to Shape Up," *Newsweek*, May 23, 1977, pp. 78 - 86.

87. Kennedy, J.C., and R.J. Hawkins, "Breaststroker's Knee," *Swimming World*, June 1974, p. 55 (reprinted from *The Physician and Sportsmedicine Magazine*).

88. ———, "Swimmer's Shoulder," *Swimming World*, August 1974, p. 26 (reprinted from *The Physician and Sportsmedicine Magazine*, April 1974).

89. Kilroy, Tom, "The Swimmer's Log—Adult Beginners," *Aquatic World*, September 1976, p. 6.

90. Langstaff, Jamie Louise, "The Metabolic and Circulatory Response to Aqua Dynamics," Applied Research Project for PED 765, University of Georgia, June 1978.

91. Lintner, Diane Marie, "Heart Rate Response to Interval Swimming at Various Percentages of Maximum Speed," Applied Research Project for PED 765, University of Georgia, August 1979.

92. Little, Mildred J., "An Inexpensive Lap-Counter for Fitness Swim Programs," in *NAGWS Aquatics Guide*, Washington, D.C.: AAHPER, 1975, p. 16.

93. Macey, Joan Mary, "Swimming as Exercise: The Better Alternative," *New York Times*, July 13, 1980.

94. Masters Swim Committee, "Swim Today—Swim for the Health of It." (Available from National AAU Masters Swim Committee, 2308 N.E. 19th Avenue, Ft. Lauderdale, FL 33305.)

95. McArdle, William D., Roger M. Glaser, and John R. Magel, "Metabolic and Cardiorespiratory Response during Free Swimming and Treadmill Walking," *Journal of Applied Physiology*, 30 (5): 733 - 738, 1971.

96. McCafferty, Bill, "Neglected Aspect of Coaching: Promoting Lifelong Fitness," *Aquatic World*, May 1976, p. 10.

97. McCue, Myra, "The Swimmer's Log—Fitness in the Water," *Aquatic World*, March 1976, p. 6.

98. McEvoy, Joseph E., "Analysis of the Individual Medley Swimming Test," doctoral dissertation, Springfield (Mass.) College, 1975.

99. ———, "Fitness Swimming—Something Old, Something New," *GAHPER (Georgia) Journal*, Winter 1979, pp. 12 - 13.

100. ———, "Portrait of a Lifetime Swimmer—Dr. Loree Florence," *Swimmer's Magazine*, September - November 1978, pp. 40 - 41.

101. ———. "Swimming For Time," *Swim Swim Magazine*, Summer, 1984, p. 20 - 21.

102. McKean, Kevin, "Exercise—72 Million Americans Can't Be Wrong—or Can They?" *Discover*, August 1982, pp. 84 - 88.

103. Morgan, William P., "Anxiety Reduction Following Acute Physical Activity," *Psychiatric Annals* 9 (3): 36 - 45, 1979.

104. ———, "Negative Addiction in Runners," *The Physician and Sportsmedicine Magazine*, 7 (2): 57 - 64, 1979.

105. Morris, Stephen N., and Paul L. McHenry, "Role of Exercise Stress Testing in Healthy Subjects and Patients with Coronary Heart Disease," *American Journal of Cardiology*, 42: 659 - 666, 1978.

106. "Motivation a Key To Participation," *Athletic Purchasing & Facilities*, July 1981, pp. 11 - 14.

107. "Ocean Racing," *Rough Water Swimming Handbook*, Summer 1981, pp. 10 - 11.

108. Pennebaker, Ruth Burney, "A 29-year-old Beginner Girds for a Long Summer," *New York Times*, July 13, 1980.

109. *The Perrier Study: Fitness in America*, conducted by Louis Harris and Associates, Inc., New York: Great Waters of France, Inc., January 1979.

110. President's Council on Physical Fitness and Sports, *Aqua Dynamics: Physical Conditioning through Water Exercises*, Washington, D.C.: U.S. Government Printing Office, 1978.

111. "Proper Uses of FFM Swim Belt," Pull-Buoy, Inc., 2511 Leach Road, Auburn Heights, Michigan 48057.

112. "Ready, Set...Sweat!" *Time*, June 6, 1977, pp. 82 – 90.

113. Recreonics Corporation, "Buyer's Guide and Operations Handbook—Catalog #35: Swimming Pool, Aquatics, and Recreational Equipment," 1983, p. 108. (Available from 1635 Expo Lane, Indianapolis, Indiana 46224.)

114. "Safety," *Rough Water Swimming Handbook*, Summer 1981, pp. 12 – 13.

115. Samuelson, Carl R., "The Making of an Olympic Champion," master's thesis, Springfield (Mass.) College, 1964.

116. Scott, Verne, "Viewpoint—Is Masters Swimming Doomed?" *Swim Swim Magazine*, Spring 1983, p. 8.

117. Seely, Scott, "Wheel of Fortune—Step Right Up and Try Your Luck," *Swimming World*, October 1977, p. 22.

118. Selye, Hans, *The Stress of Life*, New York: McGraw-Hill Book Company, 1956.

119. Silvia, Charles E., "Kinesiological Aspects of Stroke Technique," paper delivered at the American Swim Coaches Association Convention, First World Swimming Clinic, Montreal, October 1, 1971.

120. _____, *Manual and Lesson Plans for Basic Swimming, Water Stunts, Lifesaving, Springboard Diving, Skin and Scuba Diving, and Methods of Teaching*, privately published by author, March 1970.

121. _____, *Manual for Swimming, Water Stunts, Diving, Lifesaving, and Water Safety*, Tuckahoe, N.Y.: Cardinal Associates, Inc., September 1960.

122. Silvia, Charles E., and Charles J. Smith, "Springfield College Intercollegiate Swimming Team—Daily Workouts," mimeographed, October 13, 1972 – March 17, 1973.

123. Smith, C.J., and D.W. Page, "In-water Isokinesthetics," *Swimming Technique*, May 1980, p. 40.

124. *Sprint Freestyle—Men*, Aquaforums Films, P.O. Box 8, Champlain, N.Y. 12919.

125. Stern, Sol, "The New Wave in Swimming," *New York Times Magazine*, June 1, 1980, pp. 84 – 86.

126. Stoedefalke, Karl G., "Physical Fitness Programs for Adults," *American Journal of Cardiology*, 33: 787 – 789, 1974.

127. Stoedefalke, Karl G., and James L. Hodgson, "Exercise Rx—Designing a Program," *Medical Opinion*, June 1975, p. 48.

128. "Sure Stroke Wrist-Weights" (1980), Techreations, Inc., 2099 Allen Street, Springfield, MA 01128.

129. Swartz, Don, "Cyclical Training," *Swimming World*, February 1973, p. 10.

130. *Swim – Bike – Run Magazine for Multi-Sport Endurance Athletes*, Spring, 1982. (Available from 703 S. Union Avenue, Los Angeles CA 90017.)

131. *Swim Swim Magazine*, P.O. Box 5901, Santa Monica, CA 90405.

132. Welch, John H., "The Hand-Foot Concept in the Teaching and Coaching of Swimming," *Swimming Technique*, July 1965, pp. 41 – 43.

133. _____, "A Study of the Hand-Foot Concept in Swimming," master's thesis, Springfield (Mass.) College, 1959.

134. Wiener, Harvey S., *Total Swimming*, New York: Fireside Books (Simon & Schuster) 1980.

135. Williams, John H., "A National Survey of Why Women and Men Compete in Masters Championship Swimming and Diving Meets," mimeographed 1982. †

136. Young, Ron, "Wrist, Ankle and Head Weights," *Swimming World*, March 1980, pp. 36 – 38.

137. Zinman, David, "Jogging Can't Always Change a Personality," *Atlanta Journal and Constitution*, March 26, 1978.

† Bibliographic information is incomplete. Reprint of article is available from Dr. McEvoy upon request.

Note: Reprints of most articles listed above are available upon request.

171

INDEX